Afghanistan

JOHN C. GRIFFITHS

Afghanistan

WITH A HISTORICAL NOTE BY
SIR OLAF CAROE

FREDERICK A. PRAEGER, *Publishers*

New York · Washington · London

FREDERICK A. PRAEGER, *Publishers*
111 Fourth Avenue, New York, N.Y. 10003, U.S.A.
77-79 Charlotte Street, London W.1, England

Published in the United States of America in 1967
by Frederick A. Praeger, Inc., Publishers

© 1967 John C. Griffiths

Library of Congress Catalog Card Number: 67-19582

Printed in Great Britain

Dedication

*This book is for
my father, who first aroused my interest,
Ann, who let me go, and
Douglas, who made sure that I got back.*

Contents

Acknowledgements   viii

Introduction   3

1 The Pivot of Fortune   7

2 The Great Game   17

3 Red to Mate?   37

4 'Pushtunistan Unjast'   50

5 Disunity and Cohesion   65
   Who are the Afghans?; Class, Wealth and Women;
   Islam

6 An Experiment in Democracy   90
   The New Constitution; The Afghan Political Scene;
   Democratic Prospects; Administration and the Law

7 The Arithmetic of Progress   117
   Agriculture and Industry; Development Potential
   and Forward Planning

8 Prospects for the Future   135

APPENDICES

  I Historical Note by Sir Olaf Caroe   143

  II Export and Import Tables   145

  III Investment Outlay and Sources, Second Five
   Year Plan   146

  IV Constitution of Afghanistan, October 1964   147

References   170

Short Reading List   172

Index   173

MAPS

  1 Nineteenth Century: Afghanistan, and British
   and Russian expansion   ix

  2 Contemporary: Political and Communications   x–xi

Acknowledgements

My FIRST AND greatest debt is to the many, many Afghans who not only overwhelmed me with their traditional hospitality but were at great pains to answer my endless questions and to help me visit and see the things I wished to. In particular I am grateful to the Prime Minister and the many members of his Cabinet who found time to talk to me in their very busy lives, and to Mr Wala of the Ministry of Culture and Information.

I owe a debt, too, to the staff of the British Embassy in Kabul and the members of the Foreign Office who did much to help me and supply me with information and suggestions.

I am grateful to Sir Olaf Caroe and Miss Jill Thompson for reading my manuscript and making constructive comments on it; to Miss Janet Sanders and Mrs Brenda Thomas for the speed and efficiency with which they typed out the manuscript, and to Mr Derick Mirfin of the Pall Mall Press for sympathetic and valuable guidance.

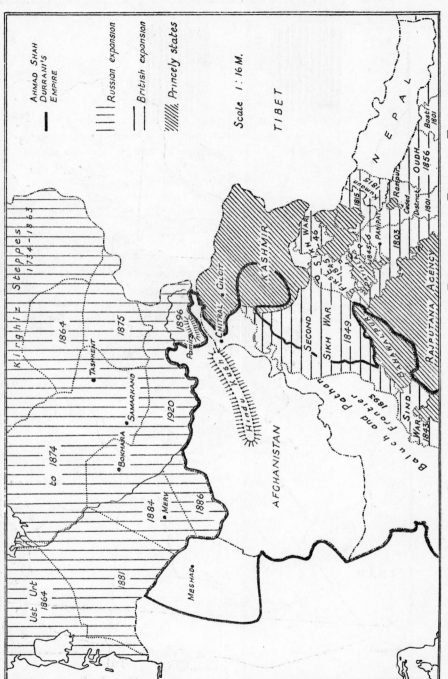

MAP 1. NINETEENTH CENTURY: AFGHANISTAN, AND BRITISH AND RUSSIAN EXPANSION

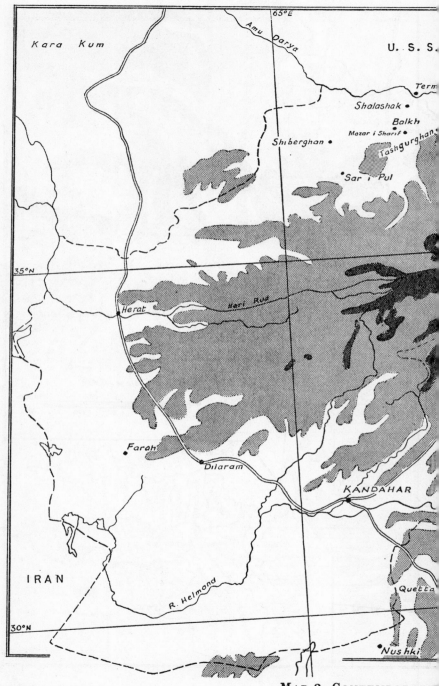

MAP 2. CONTEMPORARY

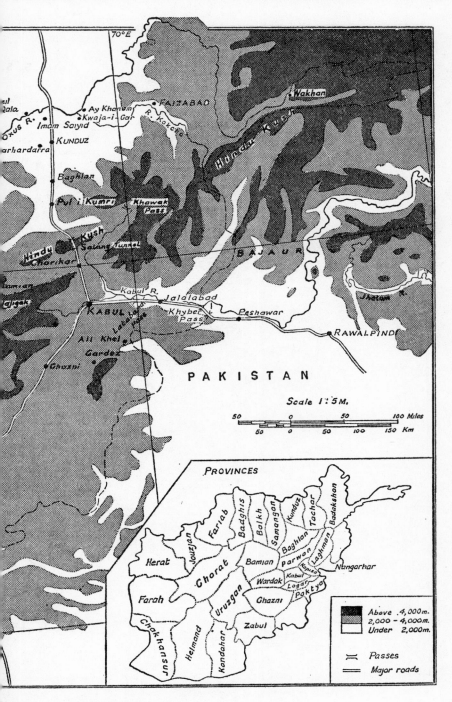

POLITICAL AND COMMUNICATIONS

Afghanistan

Introduction

ON A CLEAR June night in 1747, the army of Nadir Shah
of Persia, whose conquests had ranged from Turkey to India,
lay encamped not far from Meshed in northern Persia. Its
royal commander had decided to punish a rebellious Kurdish
tribe which had attacked his stud farm at Radkan. For this
rebellion—and it was but one of many at the time—Nadir
Shah had only his own increasing mental derangement to
blame, for it was leading him into cruelties horrifying even
by the standards of a cruel age. A French priest who accom-
panied the Shah records that 'wherever he halted, he had
many people tortured and put to death, and had towers of
their heads erected'.

Ahmad Khan, an Afghan noble in his early twenties, sat
outside his tent in the Shah's encampment, reflecting on the
circumstances that had brought him, the son of one of Nadir's
defeated opponents, into the Persian monarch's personal staff
at the age of sixteen to become, now, the commander of that
Afghan contingent, 4,000 strong, which had served in the
van of so many of the Shah's campaigns. The conquests witnessed in the company of these veterans could not fail to
inspire a young man of Ahmad Khan's temperament. He had
done well under the Shah's patronage, and it seemed permissible to dream pleasantly of the future. Sovereignty and
dominion had been prophesied for him more than once. By
the side of his tent there stood, as a token of future glory, the
little model of a royal encampment placed there by Sabir
Shah, the darvesh who had prophesied so favourably. Nadir
Shah himself had foretold that the young Afghan would be a
great king. Ahmad ruefully fingered the nick in his ear which
was the token and reminder of *that* prognostication.

3

An excited messenger from Nadir broke into his medita-
tions. Ahmad was to arm his Afghans, arrest all the officers
of the Shah's personal bodyguard in the morning, and take
over the guard duties himself. His master—always discovering plots, some real, some imagined—had that day learned of
a conspiracy against him. He had tried to flee the camp but
the guards had dissuaded him with protestations of loyalty.
Yet it was the commander of the guard who was the chief
instigator of the plot, and the Shah was taking no chances.
The conspirators were to be put in irons.

Unfortunately for the Shah, his instructions to Ahmad
were overheard by an agent of the conspirators; they realised
that their only hope lay in immediate action in anticipation
of the counterplot. Many of them backed out in the crisis, but a
handful made their way into Nadir's tent past the acquiescent
guard. One conspirator slashed off the hand that the Shah
raised to protect himself, another then struck off his head.
The murder—perhaps tyrannicide would be a fairer word—
had to be kept secret from the Afghan and Uzbeg troops so
that these could be taken unawares in the morning. But
Ahmad Khan was to benefit from having a friend in the right
place. One of Nadir Shah's widows was able to get a message
to him about the attack. Such a thing seemed incredible; even
so, Ahmad stood his men to arms all night and at first light
ordered them to the Shah's tent to establish the accuracy of
the report. At the women's quarters further advance was
barred by the Turkmen guards who were plundering the camp
indiscriminately, but the Afghans fought their way through
to learn for themselves that they had been told the truth.

By now, the gallimaufry of disparate tribal contingents
was seizing the chance to settle old scores. A dozen minor
battles flared throughout the camp. In the confusion of Nadir
Shah's instantly disintegrating empire, Ahmad and his
followers hacked their way out of the camp and began their
march home—taking the fabulous Koh-i-Noor diamond with
them. By the time they neared their destination, Kandahar,
the members of the Afghan force, drawn from a variety of
tribes, had reached the conclusion that they now owed no

allegiance to a Persian suzerain and should claim independence under their own elected chief. But who was this chief to be? The story has it that for eight long sessions they debated the matter, during all of which time Ahmad Khan said not a word. Then, in the ninth session, as the argument slackened through sheer weariness, the darvesh Sabir Shah jumped to his feet to advance Ahmad Khan's claims. 'Why all this verbosity? God has created Ahmad Khan a much greater man than any of you. His is the most noble of all the Afghan families. Maintain, therefore, God's work, for His wrath will weigh heavily on you if you destroy it.' While this account may seem an unlikely tale, clearly Ahmad Khan—or Ahmad Shah Durr-i-Durran (Pearl of Pearls) as he now became*—had already made a great impression on his fellow Afghans by his ability and personality. This impression he was quickly to enhance by his subsequent actions.

No sooner had Ahmad entered Kandahar than he managed to seize a treasure caravan of tribute bound for Nadir Shah. This he generously and shrewdly distributed among the Afghan chiefs. It was also psychologically astute of him to give the new name of Durrani to his own tribe, the Abdali, thus identifying them with himself and not with past feuds, quarrels and jealousies. In the course of the next twenty-six years, his military and political genius was to create an Afghanistan that was, for the first time, a distinct political entity in Central Asia, and a clearly recognisable progenitor of present-day Afghanistan. (See Map 1, page ix.)

---

* Doubtless under the influence of his Persian patron Nadir Shah, Ahmad adopted the title 'Shah', and his descendants continued so to style themselves until, after the civil wars at the start of the nineteenth century, the Muhammadzai dynasty came to the throne. The first Muhammadzai ruler, Dust Muhammad, styled himself 'Amir'. His descendants followed suit until, early in the twentieth century, Habibullah added 'Shah' to his titles. These historic titles are not, however, always used with nicety by foreign writers on Afghanistan. The proper title for the head of state today, dating from the proclamation of 1929 by the Muhammadzai Barakzai monarch, Nadir Shah, is 'King'. The full style of the present ruler, as set forth in the constitution of 1964 is: 'His Majesty Muhammad Zahir Shah, the King of Afghanistan'.

Afghanistan

To begin an account of modern Afghanistan with a description of the events and outcome of a single night may seem a little odd. But that June night in 1747 is much more than a dramatic adventure in the life of a tribal chief. It not only typifies the treachery, brutality and intrigue which are commonplace in so much of Afghan history; it also marks a watershed in Afghanistan's development. On the one side, there are the two thousand years and more in which the country was washed over by the sedimentary ethnic tides of invasion after invasion, and during which it—or various parts of it—formed only provinces of extensive empires. On the other side, there is the simultaneous expansion of the European powers in Asia and the growth, albeit gradual, of national consciousness in Afghanistan itself.

The problems which faced Ahmad Shah—the judicious and equitable distribution of limited wealth, the unification of naturally heterogeneous peoples, the balance between freedom and stable rule, subservience to suzerain powers—have been, in various forms, the major problems of Afghanistan during the two centuries since his reign. It is with the modern versions of these problems and the way in which Ahmad Shah's successors are now tackling them that this book is chiefly concerned.

1

The Pivot of Fortune

THE TWO THOUSAND and more years of violent and exciting history which preceded the advent of Ahmad Shah could have had no more striking and appropriate stage for their enactment than Afghanistan, for on this country the fortunes of many a great conqueror have pivoted.

Afghans are first referred to as a people in the tenth century AD, but as the tribal inhabitants of certain parts of the country now known as Afghanistan rather than as 'nationals' of the whole country. In the eighteenth and nineteenth centuries, Afghans themselves would have talked of their own regions by tribal names, and any references to the larger area would probably have been to 'Pushtun'. It is only through Persian and English writers that the term 'Afghanistan', and indeed of 'Afghans', first came into general usage, due to the fact that the ruling house was Afghan. Throughout this book, the people of Afghan race are denoted by the Indian word 'Pathans'. To call them 'Pushtuns' would imply that they *all* speak Pushtu—which is not the case. The term 'Afghans' is here made to refer to all citizens of modern Afghanistan, not solely to that racial group to which the term strictly applies. It must be borne in mind that in earlier times no members of the other racial groups would have dreamed of calling themselves Afghans.

The country of the Afghans is one of sharp contrasts in climate, terrain and people. It abounds in deserts of every kind, in the midst of which the traveller comes with eye-catching suddenness on green and fertile valleys or a confetti of purple flowers scattered across seemingly arid soil. In summer he may encounter a heat that seems to make the very flesh singe, while in winter a scimitar wind guards the snow-blocked

7

passes of the mountains that cover so much of the country.

The people vary greatly in stature, colour, race and feature: the ethnic sediment deposited in the tidal wake of at least two thousand years of invasions, sweeping by along the break-water of the Hindu Kush mountains and towards India. The Hindu Kush cuts Afghanistan virtually in half, running from the thin strip of inaccessible mountains in the north-east that barely separates Russia, China and Pakistan, almost to the empty desert sands of the western border with Iran. South and south-east lie Kandahar, Ghazni and Kabul: to the north Faizabad and Mazar-i-Sharif, and to the west Herat. North-ward of these towns, the river Oxus forms much of the border with Russia. In the south of the country, the people are mainly Pathans; in the north, Tajiks, Turkmen and Uzbegs; and in the central mountains, Hazaras.

*

Every landward invasion—save for that of the Arabs, in the eighth century of our era, through the then much more fertile Makran—has pivoted on the south-western end of the Hindu Kush or has filtered, in season, through its high passes. This has given to Herat, Kandahar and Kabul a continental strategic significance. The pattern of invasion and empire has been markedly repetitive. The impulse of the first irresistible thrust south or east; a pivot on the south-western flank of the Hindu Kush; a brief pause to conquer and consolidate some such vantage point as Ghazni or Kabul; a sweep down into India and a battle in the first open country beyond the Indus to establish a seat in northern India itself; and then the gradual softening of the conquerors in the enervating climate until they can no longer resist new incursors pressing behind them or are overthrown for a brief interregnum by a locally nurtured dynasty—such, for two millennia, has been the oft-repeated experience of those over whom the endless armies swept.

Sir Olaf Caroe in his history of the Pathans lists no less than twenty-five dynasties ruling over all or part of what is now Afghanistan, from the Achaemenian dominion of Cyrus and Darius the Great in the sixth century BC to the present ruling house of the Barakzai. In the first millennia of this period, Persian influence was not merely dominant but well-nigh exclusive, for most even of those invaders who were not themselves Persian had undergone the transmutation of contact with Persian culture through either submission or conquest. This Persian influence still pervades Afghan life today and is perhaps quite as important as the later influence of Islam.

Of all the conquests of the land of the Afghans, none can match—in military genius, at least—that of Alexander the Great who, in the four years between the battle of Gaugamela in 331 BC and the onset of his Indian campaign from its base at Alexandria Arachosia (Charikar), conquered the peoples of Khurasan, Transoxiana and what we now call Afghanistan. He left behind him Greek-garrisoned cities, many bearing his name, which he hoped would be centres of civilised and ordered dominion. Alexander's hopes were not to be fulfilled. He conquered but could not subdue these Central Asian peoples; and no sooner had he died than his lieutenants, the new Hellenistic rulers of the old Persian satrapies, fell out among themselves. None of them was strong enough to achieve an overall control, although Hellenistic kingdoms—such as that of the Seleucids and Graeco-Bactrians—were to survive in small parts of the area for a few more years.

The significance of Alexander's invasion lies not so much in its military accomplishments, or even in the social influence which, superficially at least, it appears to have had,* as in its reversal, for the first time, of the common flow of conquest from the East to the West. Although the sweeping invasions of the hordes of Central Asia were still to come, from now on the peoples of the Mediterranean and the mainland of Europe could turn their eyes eastward, not just to watch

* This influence seems to have been rather harshly underestimated by some writers. The lay-out of villages and towns on the Greek pattern, and the very prevalence of the first name 'Sikander' or 'Iskander', speak of a more profound impact than may at first be apparent. For recently discovered evidence of the Greek phase in Afghanistan's history, see the footnote about the Ay Khanum excavations, page 41 below.

for the dust clouds of invasion, but to dream of plunder, profit and glory for themselves.

The Macedonians were ousted by the only empire in this first millennium of our story to owe nothing to the Persians: the Maurya empire of Chandragupta in India. Under his grandson Asoka, Maurya rule in the second century BC spread the influence of Buddhism throughout this part of Asia. Little evidence, however, of that faith remains in Afghanistan today, save for the great rock-carvings of Bamian which even the ravages of Genghis Khan could not destroy.

Two other dynasties are worth noting, prior to the coming of Islam. The Graeco-Bactrian empire of Demetrius and Menander centred on Taxila (185–97 BC), though enduring for less than a hundred years, nurtured one of the great artistic flowerings of the ancient world: the sculptures of Gandhara. Although it now appears that many of the accomplishments of Gandharan art were achieved under the following Kushan dynasty, the impetus for this beautiful fusion of Greek and Buddhist art stems from the earlier empire. In the fifth century AD, Bactria was overrun by the White Huns: men of Turkic origin, tall and white-skinned. Checked momentarily by the Sassanid empire in Persia, by the end of the century the White Huns had not only made that empire tributary to their own but had also mastered northern India, where their rule endured well into the sixth century of our era. They proved to be the pathfinders for further invaders from Central Asia.

Contrary to what some Afghan historians would have us believe, Afghanistan was not immediately converted to Islam as soon as the Prophet breathed the word. In fact, the first Muslim régime to control a considerable part of the country (and even then it was fully effective only south of the Hindu Kush) was the Ghaznavid kingdom. The town and province of Ghazni formed a part of the Persian Samanid empire and was governed for them by a series of Turkish mamluks. Sabuktagin, who served the last of these, overthrew his master in 977 and founded the dynasty which he named after the town. Under his son Mahmud it did, indeed, achieve considerable military and cultural renown, but like so many others it was shortlived. But it was in Mahmud's reign that Islam was forcibly made the religion of Afghanistan. Ghazni was sacked in 1150 by the otherwise undistinguished (if vainglorious) Tajik, Alauddin Jahansoz—the World Burner as he liked to be called. For a brief period, rule over the Ghaznavid empire was borne by the forebears of the present Afghan Tajiks. It is not difficult to understand why these mild people, now for the most part peaceful farmers in the country round Kabul, were brushed aside by the Mongol hordes. Ghazni was destroyed again by Genghis Khan, seventy years after Alauddin Jahansoz, and today the town itself, save for the remaining Ghaznavid minarets, is only an unimpressive collection of rather dilapidated mud buildings.

Before reaching Ghazni in 1221–22, Genghis Khan had already done more razing and ravaging than any man in history before him. Fraser-Tytler in his history of Afghanistan does not much exaggerate when he says that 'the Mongol invasions of Central Asia and Europe were, until the rise of the Nazis under Hitler, the greatest catastrophe which has befallen mankind'.[1] In 1220, Genghis Khan crossed the Oxus and sacked the city of Herat, which lies on an open road fifty miles from the present Russian border. He then advanced on the ancient centre of arts and learning in Balkh, so completely devastating this area that the Moroccan traveller Ibn Batuta in 1333, more than a century later, found only rubble and desolation where there had once been great cities. Ghazni itself fell to the lot of Genghis Khan's son Chagatai but he never visited or took interest in this outpost of his domain which, as a centre of arts and learning, had been irrevocably destroyed. But, with ironic justice, the Mongols were to leave even less trace of their achievements, if that is the right word, than did the kingdoms they laid waste. The only enduring, positive witness to their presence are the colonies of Mongol Hazaras* in west-central Afghanistan: a land of narrow

* Some scholars have recently suggested that the Hazaras are not descended from the hordes of Genghis Khan but from earlier Mongol incursions.

valleys, rugged blocks of mountains and swift turbulent rivers, in keeping with the nature of the inhabitants who are aggressive and constantly at odds with the other peoples of the country.

Yet Afghanistan, reduced to an even more complete state of anarchy than usual, had not yet done with the Mongols, or at least with a Turco-Iranian branch of them. In 1379, Tamerlane crossed the Oxus by a bridge of boats at Termez, one of the few practicable points; nineteen years later, his cavalry crossed the Khawak pass en route for India. In Afghanistan itself, he even mounted a campaign against the tribesmen in the wild and mountainous country north-east of Kabul. Termed 'Kafirs' by the Muslim faithful, their land 'Kafiristan'—the Land of the Unbelievers—is now, since they embraced Islam at sword point in 1895, more felicitously known as Nuristan—the Land of Light. It was on this campaign that Tamerlane and his men tobogganed recklessly down a mountainside on their shields to attack the enemy!

Tamerlane's was a very different empire from that of his Mongol predecessors, based as it was on Samarkand—so richly and beautifully embellished by the buildings and works of art commissioned by the lame conqueror. Other cities, like Herat, became flourishing centres of the arts under his immediate successors. It was the determination to regain Samarkand and restore its glories that obsessed Babur—descended from both Tamerlane and Genghis Khan—before he realised that the ambition was a hopeless one, and instead turned his thoughts towards India. Although for many years after the loss of his kingdom in Ferghana Babur still pursued his youthful dreams, in the end the relentless logic of the southward advance of the Uzbegs under Shaibani Khan forced him to seek a kingdom in Kabul and the lands beyond the Indus. Shaibani Khan bequeathed to Afghanistan the Uzbeg people still living in the northern part of the country, while Babur went on to found one of the world's most magnificent empires, that of the Mogul dynasty in India.

For once, Kabul fell into a new ruler's hands without a

struggle, in October 1504.* 'So, towards the end of [this] month', wrote Babur in his memoirs, 'by the blessing of Almighty God I obtained and subjected Kabul and Ghazni with their provinces without effort or battle.'[2] (If Babur made history on the grand scale, he also wrote it with the delightful personal touch we find in the *Baburnama*.) He clearly recognised the strategic advantages of Kabul. Successful raids on India might be made from any centre in southern Afghanistan, but Kabul must be securely held for the permanent conquest of northern India. ('Indian' empires of the various Asiatic conquerors never had sufficient impetus to embrace the whole of southern India.) Yet for Babur the attractions of Kabul—which, as one legend has it, was founded by and named after Cain—were far more than that of mere strategic advantage. 'From Kabul', wrote Babur, 'you can go in a single day to a place where the snow never falls, and in two hours you can also reach a place where the snow never melts, except at times in a particularly hot summer.'[3] The qualification shows the typical realism of the man who saw that Kabul was 'a land to be governed by the sword, not the pen'.

That twenty-one years elapsed between Babur's capture of Kabul and his conquest of India in December 1525, with an army of less than 12,000 men, was due to the difficulty of consolidating his base from Kandahar to Kabul. This proved a laborious task in the face of the hostility of the hill tribes: those men whom Ibn Batuta had described as 'a tribe of Persians called Afghans. They hold mountains and defiles, possess considerable strength, and are mostly highwaymen.'[4] Indeed, it may be that the decision to turn his attention to building up an empire in India was influenced by his inability to subdue completely the Pathan Babur's tribesmen. These, he realised, he might contain but never control. The turbulent and independent spirit of these tribal peoples is one of the great constants of Afghanistan's history. They seem to have changed little, despite the many invasions, since the time of Alexander.

* The fact that Babur's uncle, Ulugh Beg, had held the city for thirty-two years, until 1501, may account in part for the ease of its capture.

However this may be, Babur finally penetrated into north India, and at much-embattled Panipat, site of so many contests for the mastery of India, gained the brilliant and decisive victory which was to give him the throne of Delhi. By placing the centre of his empire in that city, he made Afghanistan once more the northern outpost of an Indian empire, as in the days of the Maurya dynasty, and with the inevitable debilitating consequences. The Mogul succession in India was dramatically, if only temporarily, interrupted by Sher Shah—probably the most outstanding of the many Afghans to have carved out kingdoms away from their native land. (Sher Shah himself reigned in Delhi for only six years—from 1539 to 1545; his successors for a further ten years.) Although the reign of Babur's son Humayun was shaken for only a few years, he and his greater descendants were never able to establish complete control over Afghanistan, much of which eventually came once more under the influence of Persia.

Then, little more than two hundred years ago there arose, in the manner described in the Introduction, the first indigenous Afghan ruler of Afghanistan: Ahmad Shah Durrani.

*

Ahmad Shah's principal objective was to unite the various Afghan peoples. He realised that this unity could be achieved only by a loosely-knit system—a sort of feudal federalism—in which the independent prerogatives of the tribal chiefs would remain unimpugned by the central power provided they gave it military support. At the same time, it was at least partly to guard against possible rivals that he appointed prominent members of his family to important posts, which became virtually hereditary: a practice not unknown in modern Afghanistan. He went a step further, and constituted a Majlis (or council) of nine chiefs which played a genuinely influential part in policy-making. Though he could, and did, deal severely with the more blatant and persistent offenders against his régime, he also gained a reputation for remarkable clemency in an age not renowned for that virtue in Asia.

The second major instrument of Ahmad Shah's policy of

unification was the age-old device of foreign conquest. This
has been well described by Mountstuart Elphinstone in his
perceptive *Account of the Kingdom of Caubul.*

For the consolidation of his power at home he relied in
great measure on the effects of his foreign wars. If these
were successful, his victories would raise his reputation,
and his conquests would supply him with the means of
maintaining an army, and of attaching the Afghan chiefs
by favour and rewards; the hopes of plunder would induce
many tribes to join him, whom he could not easily have
compelled to submit; by carrying the great men with his
army he would be able to prevent their increasing, or even
preserving, their influence in their tribes; and the habits of
military obedience would prepare them for a cheerful submission to his government at home; the troops also, having
the King constantly before their eyes, and witnessing the
submission of their hereditary chiefs, would learn to regard
him as the head of the nation; and he might hope, as the
event proved, that his popular manners, and the courage,
activity, vigilance and other military virtues which he
possessed, would impress all ranks with respect, and
strongly attach his soldiers to his person.[5]

Ahmad Shah's first step after taking power in Kandahar in
1747 was to subdue Kabul, and Ghazni en route. Before the
end of the year, less than six months after coming to power,
he had set out on the first of those eight invasions of India
that were to fulfil so successfully the policy described by
Elphinstone.

However, fortunately for the future of his own country, he
had no ambition or desire, as had so many previous invaders
of the subcontinent, to transfer his seat of government to
Delhi and to rule India. Ahmad Shah's interest was in conquest, not empire, and after his campaigns he always returned
to Kabul. It is doubtful whether he could have maintained
his kingdom from a capital in Delhi. Afghanistan at this time
was fortunately relieved of external pressures by the disintegration earlier in the century of the Mogul and the Persian

Safavid empires, and the Sikhs had not yet become established. Although Ahmad Shah generally defeated his Indian opponents (principally Sikhs and Marathas) in battle, they flowed in again like puddle water behind his wagon wheels as soon as he marched on. He could not maintain permanent lines of communication across territory still in the hands of such formidable opponents. He returned to his own country after each invasion to consolidate his domestic position and to extend the other frontiers of his empire. In the early years of his reign he added to his dominions Khurasan, Bamian and Badakshan.

When Ahmad Shah died at the age of fifty, from a particularly unpleasant combination of diabetes and an ulcerating nose wound, the old-style internecine struggle for power immediately broke out again among his sons, and gradually his empire crumbled. But he had carved out a kingdom which, he showed, did have certain elements of cohesion. Save for its tenuously held regions in Khurasan and east of the Khyber, in the Punjab and southwards in Baluchistan and Sind, Ahmad Shah's realm covered, broadly speaking, the area of present-day Afghanistan. That it required external compression, to be applied by the advancing empires of Britain and Russia, to make these elements of cohesion ultimately effective, is the next major part of Afghanistan's history.

2

The Great Game

WITH THE FOUNDING of the Mogul empire by Babur, the
centuries of pre-eminence of the horse-bowmen of Central
Asia came to an end. Not until the Chinese incursion of 1962
would India again be invaded from Central Asia. But, if the
great subcontinent was now secure from attack from the
north, at the courts of the great Mogul emperors there appeared
—outwardly diffident and deferential, at heart observant,
curious and ambitious—the outriders of a far more powerful
invasion from a different direction and of a different kind.

By the mid-eighteenth century, at the time when the
Afghans were forming their first independent kingdom under
Ahmad Shah, the British were establishing themselves firmly,
under the aegis of the East India Company, in substantial
parts of India. As mercantile interests developed into political
involvement, so this latter engendered a British military
presence, first in conflict with the rival power of France and
its Indian allies and then, after the defeat of France, with the
native principalities themselves. Thus the British found
themselves constantly obliged to extend the areas under their
military control in order to maintain the stability necessary
for prosperous trade. The British advance towards the frontiers
of Afghanistan, by means both of diplomacy and war, cul-
minated in the first and second Sikh wars (1845 and 1849).
These, by breaking the power of Ranjit Singh's successors,
brought British rule right up to the borders of Afghanistan.

Nor was Britain alone in extending its power towards
Afghanistan, although Russia's expansion to its south-east
did not get under way until almost a generation after the
consolidation of the British presence in northern India.
During the first half of the nineteenth century, the Russians

17

were engaged in taking over the Kirghiz steppes, and were still a long way from their present frontiers with Afghanistan. Their ventures in this part of the world had to be conducted at second hand. In 1838, they persuaded the Persians to lay siege to the strategically situated city of Herat. The implications of this seemed clear. A British diplomat with the Persian army, who was trying to persuade the Shah to abandon the project, observed in a report: 'The fall of Herat would destroy our position in Afghanistan and place nearly all that country under the influence or authority of Russia and Persia.'[1] However, the defence of Herat, courageously conducted under the leadership of a young British lieutenant* who had just arrived in the city, was stubborn and the city held out until Britain's threat of war forced the Shah to break off the operation and withdraw his army, thus temporarily thwarting Russian ambitions in the area.

Russia's aims at the time were mainly commercial, if a despatch from Count Nesselrode (October 20, 1838), the Russian Foreign Minister, to his ambassador in London is to be believed. It refers to the

. . . indefatigable activity displayed by English travellers in spreading disquiet among the people of Central Asia, and in carrying agitation even into the heart of the countries bordering on our frontiers; while on our part we ask nothing but to be admitted to [share] in fair competition the commercial advantages of Asia. English industry, exclusive and jealous, would deprive us entirely of the benefits which it [claims] to reap alone; and would cause, if it could, the produce of our manufacturers to disappear from all the markets of Central Asia.[2]

Lord Auckland, the Governor-General of India at this period, imperfectly appreciated the significance of events in Afghanistan or the importance of at least a prophylactic friendship with Dust Muhammad in countering Russian ambitions.

* Eldred Pottinger, whose exciting subsequent career, before dying young of a fever, included survival of the retreat from Kabul in 1842 and—with one other man only—of the massacre at Charikar which immediately preceded it.

The Great Game

The Dust, as he was known to the British, was an able ruler who had emerged from the anarchy of the first quarter of the nineteenth century. He ousted the Saddozai descendants of Ahmad Shah to become the first of the Barakzai clan to hold the throne. Anxious though he was to secure British friendship, he never met with the response he deserved from the Raj.

Auckland embarked on an intrigue with the Sikh leader, Ranjit Singh, to place a puppet ruler, Shah Shuja, on the Afghan throne. He thus launched Britain on the first of the three Afghan wars that were to prove so disastrous for its relations with Afghanistan.* Shah Shuja was set up in 1839 with an ease that was surprising—and also deceptive, for the British suffered a crushing defeat at Afghan hands three years later, in 1842, through the sheer stupidity of the men on the spot. By the autumn of that year Kabul was retaken and the British, with no puppet to dangle once more on its throne, rather pettily burned down the Great Bazaar in Kabul. By the first Afghan war, Britain had aroused a heritage of hatred and distrust which has perhaps not entirely been dispelled from Afghan minds even to this day, although its extent can be exaggerated.

*

There followed seventy years of vacillation in British policy for, even in the high noon of expansionism in the latter half of the nineteenth century, there were strong differences of opinion regarding Afghanistan. Things looked very different from the respective vantage points of London and Delhi, while the changes of political power in England between half-hearted Imperialists and ill-informed Liberals made the pursuit of a consistent policy almost impossible.

Those—like Lord Roberts and the Duke of Cambridge—who favoured an active British presence in Afghanistan supported what came to be known as the 'Forward policy', which accepted the logic of imperial necessity. India could not be defended along its existing frontiers, hence it was essential—

* For a more 'positive' appreciation of the first and second Afghan wars, see Sir Olaf Caroe's Note, Appendix I.

so the argument ran—to push those frontiers forward to the natural barrier of the Hindu Kush. Only thus could authority and jurisdiction over the wild frontier tribes be established, the Afghans be convinced of the advisability of throwing in their lot with the British, and the Indian empire be secured. Had the Forward policy been put fully into operation in an avowedly imperialist mood, it is at least arguable that the stability of the area would today be greater than it is. But Liberal opinion rejected this policy outright, chiefly because of its belief that aggressive wars were morally indefensible; and also, perhaps, in reaction to the secondary arguments of the Forward school, such as that control of the tribal areas would provide the British army with a new recruiting source of good fighting men, loyal cannon-fodder for the Raj.

When in power, the Liberals tried to reverse decisions and dispositions made in the name of the Forward policy, some of them going so far as to suggest that, if a natural frontier were required for India, Britain would do well to withdraw to the Indus.* They did not perhaps fully appreciate the bloody consequences of such a withdrawal. The hill tribesmen, left to their own devices, would take their traditional road of plunder and depredation, and this in all probability would provoke the traditional response of brutal reprisals and punitive expeditions. Even so, it was Liberal opinion which, by promoting the concept of a buffer state, was to some extent responsible for the creation of modern Afghanistan— although one need not go so far as Sir Thomas Holdich who, at the turn of the century, wrote:

> We have contributed much to give a national unity to that nebulous community which we call Afghanistan (but which Afghans never call by that name) by drawing a boundary

* In view of the criticism of this Liberal advocacy of the southerly 'realistic' frontier on the Indus, it is only fair to note that this policy was not simply a notion dreamed up in remote London by what Imperialists called the 'Perish India' school of radicals. First suggested by Sir James Outram, the celebrated Political Agent, in 1854, the Indus frontier line was also advocated by other men on the spot, including Sir John (later Lord) Lawrence, Governor-General, 1863–68.

all round it and elevating it into the position of a buffer state between ourselves and Russia.

What is there about Afghanistan to guarantee its continued existence as a buffer state between England and Russia? No other country in the world is interested in its prolonged existence except these two. Afghanistan, as a national entity, can only exist by favour of military support of one or the other of them. We need hardly enquire on which side the burden will always lie.[3]

There is a nice irony in this last remark.

During the second half of the nineteenth century, the Russians moved inexorably southward into Central Asia under the leadership of such brilliant generals and administrators as Kaufman and Skobelev. The logic and justification of this advance was set out in a memorandum of the Russian Chancellor, Prince Gorchakov, in 1864. In a different geographical context, it might have come from the pen of a British minister.

The position of Russia in Central Asia is that of all civilised states which come into contact with half savage, wandering tribes possessing no fixed social organisation.

It invariably happens in such cases that the interests of security on the frontier, and of commercial relations, compel the more civilised states to exercise a certain ascendancy over neighbours whose turbulence and nomad instincts render them difficult to live with. First we have incursions and pillage to repress. In order to stop these, we are compelled to reduce the tribes on our frontier to a more or less complete submission. Once this result is attained they become less troublesome, but in their turn they are exposed to the aggression of more distant tribes. The state is obliged to defend them against these depredations and to chastise those who commit them. Hence the necessity of distant and costly expeditions, repeated at frequent intervals, against an enemy whose whole social organisation enables him to elude pursuit. If we content ourselves with chastising the freebooters and then retire, the lesson is soon forgotten. Retreat is ascribed to weakness, for Asiatics respect only visible and palpable force; that arising from the exercise of reason and a regard for the interests of civilisation has as yet no hold over them. The task has, therefore, to be performed over again. The United States in America, France in Algeria, Holland in her colonies, England in India—all have been inevitably drawn to a course wherein ambition plays a smaller part than imperious necessity and where the greatest difficulty is knowing where to stop.[4]

Soon Britain also was to return full-bloodedly to the Forward policy which had been in abeyance as a consequence of the Indian Mutiny of 1857 and of the prevalence of Liberal attitudes at home. In 1876, Disraeli appointed Lord Lytton to be Viceroy of India, with a clear brief to reinstate the Forward policy. A memorandum of instructions clearly summarised the situation Lytton was sent to change, and he was asked to consider 'the probable influence of that situation upon the uncertain character of an oriental chief whose ill-defined dominions are thus brought within a steadily narrowing circle between the conflicting pressures of two great military empires, one of which expostulates and remains passive, while the other apologises and continues to move forward'.[5]

As a result of Lytton's close adherence to his instructions, Britain was soon embroiled in a second Afghan war (1878–79). This was successful militarily, a swiftly moving campaign leading to the capture of such key points as Kabul and Kandahar. Indeed, in 1879 or 1880, the British very likely could have taken over the control and administration of Afghanistan south of the Hindu Kush, thereby bringing the Forward policy, of which Lytton was so staunch a supporter, to its logical conclusion. Yet Disraeli's Viceroy got cold feet and looked for a way out of assuming for Britain *de facto* responsibility for the area. Although an ardent Forwardist, in the first three months of 1880 Lytton realised that his speculative plans for breaking up Afghanistan could only involve the same tragic disasters as those experienced in Lord Auckland's time, and would also place an intolerable burden on both Treasury and Army. He perhaps now recognised, as so many others had before him, the difference between defeating and controlling the Afghan tribes.

The change in policy was finally clinched when Gladstone defeated Disraeli in the election of March 1880 and sent the Marquess of Ripon to replace Lytton as Viceroy. Indeed, British policy towards Afghanistan had been a major issue in the election, and the Liberal 'regressive' view had been eloquently put by Gladstone in one of his Midlothian speeches:

> Remember, the sanctity of life in the hill villages of Afghanistan among the winter snows is as inviolable in the eye of almighty God as can be your own. Remember that He who has united you as human beings in the same flesh and blood, has bound you by the law of mutual love, is not limited by the shores of this island, is not limited by the bounds of Christian civilisation; that it passes over the whole surface of the earth, and embraces the meanest along with the greatest in its unmeasured scope.[6]

With the Conservative defeat, it was these impeccable—if rather generalised—sentiments which became the motivating force behind British policy in India and displaced the Forward policy. Writing to the new Viceroy in May 1880, Lord Hartington, Secretary of State for India in the new Gladstone administration, was terse and to the point in his estimate of what had been gained by the second Afghan war:

> Thus it appears that as the result of two successful campaigns, of the employment of an enormous force, and of the expenditure of large sums of money, all that has yet been accomplished has been the disintegration of the state which it was desired to see strong, friendly and independent, the assumption of fresh and unwelcome liabilities in regard to one of its provinces, and a condition of anarchy throughout the remainder of the country.[7]

It was fortunate for Britain that at this juncture there came to the Afghan throne one of its greatest occupants: Abdurrahman, one of the few men who could have restored the measure of stability to Afghanistan so essential to British policy. By 1881, the policy of the buffer state was again in operation, applied by a Liberal government in the hope, rather than the assurance, that the Afghans would resist the Russians as vigorously as they had the British. Such conflict as there was between the great powers was still at second hand, as at Herat forty years earlier, only now it was a British protégé who was worsted when the Russians, in 1885, after occupying the oasis of Merv in the previous year, soundly defeated a large Afghan army barring their final advance up to the river Oxus.

On the last day of March of that year, the Russians attacked and seized the Afghan-held Panjdeh oasis at the very time when London and St Petersburg were negotiating the precise demarcation of the new frontier between Russia and Afghanistan. That this was not intended to be the final Russian goal was made quite clear in the newspaper *Novosti* shortly afterwards. Herat lay within temptingly easy grasp, and *Novosti* urged that Russia must press on to occupy the city and so 'pierce a window' looking south-eastwards, a convenient halting place for a still further advance towards the Indian Ocean in fulfilment of Russia's 'historic destiny'. The tsarist government may well have reckoned that, with the anti-imperialist Liberals in power in Britain, it could steal a march on the negotiations, and gain a useful strategic position, by a coup de force. If so, they were deceived. Gladstone sought for and obtained from Parliament a war credit of £11 million. For several weeks it seemed possible that Britain would go to war with Russia; but eventually the latter climbed down. The diplomats of the two countries returned to their task of defining the boundaries of the Amir of Afghanistan's dominions: a definition which, in fact, gave Panjdeh to the Russians in exchange for various salients of territory on the Amir's side of the Oxus.

Nothing gives a clearer indication of where the real sovereignty of Afghanistan lay at this time than these and later boundary negotiations between Britain and Russia. The Afghans were mere spectators, while the government of the Chinese empire refused to take part in the boundary demarcation discussions in 1895 over the small area of the Wakhan affecting its border. From 1889, the British and Chinese governments had been resisting Russian incursion into the Pamirs, a mountainous region (the 'Roof of the World') where the two new empires in Asia met the oldest surviving empire of the continent at the north-western extension of the Tibetan tableland. The Pamir Convention of 1895 between Britain and Russia settled the Wakhan question to the satisfaction of London and St Petersburg, and official circles there felt small concern at the absence of an endorsement of the new demarcation by the government of the decaying Chinese empire. It was not until November 1963 that Peking finally recognised its frontier with Afghanistan as determined by the Pamir Convention—thereby surrendering the line of argument, so far as Afghanistan is concerned, that the Chinese People's Republic has adhered to in regard to the Simla Convention of 1914 which defined the Indo-Tibetan frontier but which, never formally ratified by the imperial government of China, has therefore been held invalid by the Chinese ever since. This Tibetan boundary question, product of the Simla Convention, became a *casus belli* in 1962. The Afghan boundary, demarcated by the Pamir Convention, is now unlikely to become a source of conflict between China and Afghanistan.*

An equally troublesome boundary was demarcated in 1893, equally arbitrarily, on the eastern and southern borders of Afghanistan. The Durand Line (named after the British administrator responsible for devising it) is a topographically convenient foothill boundary which cuts right across ethnic and tribal divisions.† This political severance of the Pathan tribes on either side of it—a severance they have been inclined

---

* It should be noted, however, that unconfirmed rumours in Kabul late in the summer of 1966 held that there had been some trouble over Chinese border infringements in this area.

† Some authorities question the 'arbitrary' character of the Durand Line. See Sir Olaf Caroe's Note, Appendix I.

to ignore at will—not only gave rise to a whole genre of early twentieth-century schoolboy fiction but has bitterly embroiled the governments of Pakistan and Afghanistan, between which countries the Durand Line now runs.

The planting of boundary posts on the northern frontier of Afghanistan by the joint Anglo-Russian commission was something more than a topographical exercise; it indicated the tacit if limited agreement of two mutually suspicious powers to recognise the confines of their respective spheres of influence. Thus Holdich could calmly note, having described Herat and Quetta as the two hinges of the gate to India: '. . . these two doors are locked, there is nothing in this year of grace 1900 that need cause us any apprehension for the future safety of the country'.[8]

Although the opportunity for effective exercise of any Forward policy was gone for good by the turn of the century, its advocates were still promoting it. The Hon. George Curzon, (as he then was) waxed eloquent in *The Times* shortly before becoming Viceroy of India.

> Russia has, by the Pamir Convention concluded with Great Britain, just come into possession of three fourths of the whole territory known as the Pamirs, and of a position which brings her down to the main stream of the Oxus. Locally, this involves a great extension of her military and political prestige. If at the very same moment that she is thus permitted to advance up to the Hindu Kush on the north, Great Britain voluntarily retires from a position which she has occupied for ten years on the south, but one interpretation will be placed upon this coincidence by the natives of those regions. They do not understand high diplomacy, and they do not read the letters of retired governors and generals in *The Times*. But with one alphabet they are perfectly familiar, and its two symbols are forward and backward. They will say that Russia is the winning and Britain the receding power.[9]

Lord Roberts spoke as earnestly, if less eloquently, in the House of Lords:

The forward policy, in other words the policy of endeavouring to extend our influence over, and establish law and order on, that part of the border where anarchy, murder and robbery up to the present time have reigned supreme, a policy which has been attended with the happiest results in Baluchistan and the Gilgit frontier—is necessitated by the incontrovertible fact that a great military power is now within striking distance of our Indian possessions and in immediate contact with the state, for the integrity of which we have made ourselves responsible. Some forty years ago the policy of non-interference with the tribes, so long as they did not trouble us, may have been wise and prudent, though selfish and not altogether worthy of a great civilising power.[10]

But the necessities of European politics were changing and no longer sustained the same degree of confrontation on the frontiers of Central Asia. Indeed, Russia and Britain, sharing a common fear of the growing military strength of imperial Germany in Europe and a common uneasiness over its ambitious diplomatic and commercial forays into the Near East, became allies in 1907 in association with France. The two great Asian empires settled down to administer their respective territories round the frontiers of Afghanistan in ways that sometimes were very similar and sometimes exhibited revealing differences.

One common factor, giving each imperial régime an apparently perennial vigour, was the supply line to the home country for recruitment—in Britain's case by sea, in Russia's by the network of railways reaching to the remotest corners of its southern provinces. A revolution in communications had brought about what numerous revolutions in military technology and tactics had failed to achieve. For the first time, there were now empires in this part of Asia whose rulers did not go into an enervated decline within a few generations since they were constantly refreshed by transfusions of blood kept fresh in the climatic and moral refrigerators of northern Europe. Such empires would endure, or pass away only through voluntary relinquishment.

In conception, the imperial ideals of Britain and Russia, might seem very similar. An enlightened Russian colonial administrator could write in his memoirs after the Russian annexation of Transcaspia:

> The entry of Russia into Central Asia, followed by the introduction of European methods and civilisation, brought a breath of fresh air to a land despoiled and impoverished by centuries of Asian despotic rule. The reader, accustomed to differentiate between what he has been taught to regard as Western civilisation and conditions in Russia, may fail to appreciate the magnitude and effect of the changes wrought in the life of Central Asia by tsarist and autocratic Russia. Slavery was brought to an end; the arbitrary legislation of the Khans, Emirs, and their puppets, the Beks, who controlled a large part of their masters' wealth, such as their flocks, was superseded by Russian law, under which all the inhabitants, irrespective of their standing, were equal. Hitherto enslaved captives from every race in Asia, emancipated overnight, hastened home to spread the news of these wondrous changes, introduced by a humane administration, upheld by one universal writ, and enforced by Russian arms. Henceforth, the verdicts of the *kadis* (judges) in the local courts were based on the wise adaptation of the *Shari'at* (the holy law of Islam) to the Russian conception of justice.[11]

Would a member of the Indian Civil Service have differed much from this in his description of what he believed British rule to be achieving in India?

In Russia, however, the disease of bureaucracy spread even more virulently than it did in British India. Moreover, into Russia's southern empire poured an influx of colonial settlers from the poorer and tougher sections of Russian society, and these were not going to allow any nice regard for native susceptibilities to hamper their determination to make good. Britain, in India at least, was not faced with the same problem, for there the empire-builders were in the main dedicated career-officers who returned to their own country on completing their service. The Russians tended to despise the British, in the first place for not putting their colonies to better commercial use, and secondly for not imposing outright their own laws and customs on the subject peoples. Russianise, not liberalise, was the formula for tsarist imperialism: a formula the Soviets were not reluctant to inherit. (Forty per cent of the present population of Soviet Central Asia is of Russian origin.)

By the beginning of the twentieth century, then, a military and diplomatic stalemate had been reached as if by a kind of Newtonian Third Law of politics. Between the two equal and opposite forces lay Afghanistan.

★

It was probably fortunate for the great powers bickering over Afghanistan that, during the nineteenth and much of the twentieth centuries, the country's potential leaders were pre-occupied with throne-hunting. In 1818, after a series of particularly barbaric plots and counter-plots in which the blinding of opponents was a routine feature, the successors of Ahmad Shah were ousted by the Muhammadzai Barakzai clan. The ancestor of this clan, a group within the Durrani tribe, had stood down in the leadership contest from which Ahmad Shah emerged as the chosen chief of the Afghans. It was during the disputes over the succession in the first quarter of the last century that the Punjab and Peshawar were finally lost to the Afghan kingdom. The Barakzai, a second branch of whom provides the ruling family today, had very strong emotional ties with Peshawar, the winter capital of its ancestors until wrested from them by Sikh arms. This close dynastic association with a 'lost province' was possibly in the minds of those early Victorians, like Alexander Burnes, who believed that stability in this part of the world depended on the restoration of Peshawar to the Durrani kingdom. It is a contributory factor in the persistent irredentism of subsequent Afghan monarchs.

The age-old pattern of clan, family and personal rivalry for power was aggravated by the attempts of outside powers, the British in particular, to manipulate Afghan rulers to their own ends. The importance of personal magnetism and leadership was, and is, greater in Afghanistan than in most countries. During the nineteenth century, Abdurrahman (1880–1901) was the only man of sufficient stature to negotiate with the British the kind of independence which the country now enjoys. But with Russia troubling his northern frontiers, even after the annexation of Panjdeh, he could not afford to dispense with Britain's patronage. Even so, he took good care to exclude from his kingdom, as far as possible, both British and Russian military and diplomatic representatives.

The First World War, during which the Afghans, despite the many temptations, remained neutral as they had promised, deeply undermined the foundations of genuine imperial power for Britain; while, after 1917, the new communist régime in Russia was wholly absorbed in the problems of consolidating its domestic control. Thus the Afghans found themselves free to aspire to greater independence.

To some extent, independence was achieved as a reaction from the very restraint exercised by the Amir of Afghanistan during the war. Neutrality was exceedingly irksome to a people that saw in the war an opportunity to throw off the foreign yoke, and particularly that of the British who ruled over parts of the old Afghan kingdom in the north-west of India. Moreover, there was always the excuse of going to the aid of the Caliph under attack from infidels—although such an excuse would have carried less weight in Afghanistan, rather isolated from the rest of the Muslim world, than in other Islamic countries. Hence, when Amir Habibullah was murdered in 1919, it was not difficult for his younger son Amanullah, darling of the hotheads and nationalists, and in control at the crucial moment of the key centre of Kabul, to seize power at the expense of his conservative elder brother. Amanullah, however, had an almost unlimited capacity for arousing the antagonism of the powerful conservative elements in the country, particularly the mullahs, the Muslim religious leaders. Within a very short time, he found his hold becoming precarious.

With considerable political astuteness, he launched, in May 1919, the third Afghan war with the British under the double pretext of a struggle for independence and a *Jihad*, or holy war. Although he was quickly defeated, his campaign achieved its objectives in a way that a rising between 1914–18 would have failed to do. This was the psychological moment. A war-weary, and wiser, Britain accorded full independence to Afghanistan by releasing it from all the limitations on its freedom of action in foreign affairs that had been imposed in the past. The Treaty of Rawalpindi of 1919 was followed by another in 1921 confirming the position. In the latter year, the Russians likewise signed a rather more grandiose, if less fully honoured, treaty. Amanullah was temporarily assured of his throne.

His retention of it, however, depended not on the British or the Russians but on his own people. The intemperate reforming zeal, probably stimulated by the reforms of Reza Shah in Persia, of a young man of limited ability, determined to drag his country into the twentieth century no matter how loud its protests, was too much for a society which was still living, quite contentedly, in the Middle Ages. Resistance to him took active shape in 1924, when he introduced a sweeping programme for the emancipation of women. This would not only have educated them but, even more provocative to traditionalists, would have freed them from complete domination by their menfolk. The mullahs raised the tribes in rebellion. One mullah was arrested for declaring the reforms to be against the law of Islam and for prophesying that 'when they come in, Islam will go out'. Although Amanullah's forces were eventually successful, the rebellion was brought to an end only when he agreed to allow the Loya Jirgah, the Great Assembly (a representative council of notables, not a body elected 'democratically' in the Western sense), to repeal his measures. One cannot help wondering what became of those few women who went to Europe for education and were then called back to be reincarcerated in purdah.

Amanullah had neither the power nor the personality to create an acceptable system of modern government, greatly as this was needed. A country-wide trail of derelict and useless gadgetry, costing far more than Afghanistan's limited exchequer could bear, testified depressingly to the headlong and ill-informed way he had set about an essential task. He was encouraged to resume his reckless pursuit of wholesale reform and modernisation when, late in 1927, he embarked on a splendid and extensive tour of Europe. Inspired by what he saw in more advanced countries,* on his return in the following year he proclaimed again a programme of reforms. There was to be an assembly of 150 elected representatives legislating and supervising the executive under a constitutional monarch; monogamy was to be introduced, along with compulsory and secularised education for children of both sexes. Implicit in his policy was the creation of separate 'church' and 'state' on the lines of the system developed (at the cost of much social and political strife) in some of the European countries he had visited. But such a policy, based on a distinction between the sacred and secular, was quite incomprehensibly alien in an Islamic state at that time. All this he proclaimed to an assembly of chiefs and other notables not made any more amenable by the enforced and embarrassing discomfort of surrendering their flowing tribal costume for European formal dress. Insurrection broke out again. This time, despite its unconcerted character, it continued with growing intensity until, in the ensuing disintegration of order and central authority, the throne in Kabul was seized by a brigand, a most untypical Tajik, Bachha-i-Saqao—'son of the water carrier'. Amanullah himself retreated by stages to exile in Italy.

Thus, in 1929, it looked as if Afghanistan was about to plunge yet again into one of its periods of anarchy. The Russians, who had been trying to exert influence at the Afghan court with only spasmodic success, were only too eager to exploit the situation. However, Britain, by declaring and following a policy of absolute neutrality in the struggle between the brigand usurper and his opponents, obliged Russia to do likewise. The internal struggle for power was

* Perhaps particularly by his brief encounter with Lenin in Moscow.

undertaken by indigenous protagonists alone, and it soon transpired that the most effective of these was Nadir Khan, Amanullah's kinsman and founder of the present dynasty. His main strength lay in the support given him by tribes of the frontier districts. It is significant that Nadir owed his success as much to the tribes on the British side of the Durand Line—despite the efforts of the North-West Frontier Agency to prevent his recruiting there—as to those from the Afghan side. Early in October 1929, these forces took Kabul and on the sixteenth of the month Nadir was proclaimed King with the title of Muhammad Nadir Shah.

Nadir Shah was a man of sufficiently strong personality to attract the support of the tribes. Although at first he had to rely on these turbulent and unruly followers, he was able in the next four years, by identifying himself with the conservatives and by appointing his brothers to major ministerial posts, to stabilise the country. To insure this stability, he and his successors built up the armed services in size, efficiency and prestige. The consequent potential for a military coup in a country where, apart from the tribes, there are as yet no other organised power complexes, should not be overlooked. Nadir also reconstituted the Loya Jirgah, making it a body of delegates from every tribe and province. In 1930, after the confirmation of his accession, 105 members were chosen—not of course, elected—to form a nucleus meeting more regularly to rubber-stamp the decisions of the executive. Such was Nadir Shah's conservative concession to 'modernism', in contrast to Amanullah's sweepingly radical emulation of Western institutions.

The new régime succeeded in diminishing the influence of the great powers by limiting their opportunities for operations of any kind in Afghanistan itself—whether diplomatic, military or economic—and by carefully balancing a concession to one by a concession to another. At the start of Nadir Shah's reign, the Russians crossed the Oxus into the virtually lawless northern provinces and penetrated deep into Afghan territory in pursuit of a bandit who had been harassing the Russian side from an Afghan base and whom they thought

33

the Afghans were too dilatory in bringing to justice. The incursion had the desired result of making the Afghans bring him to book themselves and, indeed, it accelerated the restoration of order and central control to the northern provinces. But soon Russian influence became as remote as British, and other Europeans—Germans in particular—began to play an increasing part in the technical development of Afghanistan.

When, four years after his succession, Nadir was assassinated by a schoolboy,* the transition of power to his son through a family regency was perfectly smooth. Throughout the 1930s, enjoying a considerable measure of internal stability, Afghanistan made its first serious steps towards economic development, particularly in communications, irrigation and the search for mineral resources. At the same time, its government refrained from overvigorous expression of its dislike for the country's imperial neighbours. Though abating in no way its reluctance in practice to recognise the Durand Line as its southern frontier with the British empire in India, Afghanistan adhered to its declared neutrality throughout the Second World War. This neutrality was of critical importance in 1940 when Britain was stretched to its utmost and Germany was lavish in its blandishments in the hope that Afghanistan could be induced to create trouble on India's North-West Frontier.

*

As in 1919, a world war and its consequences were to have important repercussions for Afghanistan. The European imperial powers in Asia were everywhere in retreat after 1945. Their victory, the repossession of the lands lost to Japan and the retention of those they had successfully defended, was to be the farewell gesture of their power. Only in Soviet Asia were the imperialists not in retreat. Indeed, the German

* The youth was a natural son of Ghulam Nabi, executed by Nadir Shah as a prominent and disaffected adherent of Amanullah. But so isolated was the assassination from political action that it was certainly motivated by personal revenge, not political conspiracy.

invasion of European Russia had accelerated the growth of industry and communications in Asiatic Russia where the Soviet authorities built up the economic 'masse de manœuvre' to defeat the Germans. While Britain's withdrawal from India in 1947 removed any remaining threat from Afghanistan's southern border, there was immediately beyond its northern border a rapidly expanding economy and modern social organisation among peoples ethnically akin to those on the Afghan side of the Oxus. To the west, only Britain's and America's expressed determination to use force if necessary had secured the withdrawal of a Russian army of occupation from northern Persia. This situation was in marked contrast to that among Afghanistan's neighbours and cousins to the south and east, among whom confusion reigned as a result of the bloody transfer of power, and who were in any case totally absorbed in the problems of trying to create a new state—Pakistan—out of nothing.

In many parts of Asia since the Second World War, the Americans have tried, more or less successfully, to fill the vacuum left by the departure of the European powers. But nothing has adequately replaced the bulwark of the British empire against a downward thrust from Central Asia towards India. A policy of determined neutralism by the new state of India, whereby aid is welcome but political and military strings are rejected; the precarious position of Pakistan despite the infusion of American arms and money; the hostility between the two successor states of the Raj, their attention and energies absorbed in divided Kashmir, the settlement of refugee claims and (until recently) the Indus Waters dispute— all this means that there is at present no subcontinental power with the effective strength to check a Soviet-inspired southward thrust should one ever materialise.

If the concept of Afghanistan's raison d'être, given classical expression by such a man as Holdich, still held true then there would today be little likelihood of the buffer state's surviving long in the face of any such southward impulse of Russia to fulfil its 'historic destiny'. Yet, twenty years after the British withdrawal from India, Afghanistan still exists as an independent state. How genuine that independence is, and to what extent the state's existence is permanent or only a transient variation in an old historical pattern, are the questions with which the remainder of this book is chiefly concerned.

3

Red to Mate?

'Turn the pointer back to zero before starting' reads
the instruction on the Russian petrol pumps which supply the
car-traveller all over northern Afghanistan. A mental re-
adjustment of a similar kind is necessary for anyone today
who bases his expectations of the country on the Afghanistan
of even a decade ago. Preconceptions of a simple and primitive
society have to go by the board—partially at least, if not
completely for, if great changes have occurred, they are
patchy in their effects. Suddenly Afghanistan has become an
incongruous blend of the old and the new, albeit one in which
the old still predominates. It is a country suspended in a
limbo between the Middle Ages and the twentieth century:
purdah and green plastic sandals; Cadillacs and Karakul
skins; the host who will beggar himself in the name of hospitality, and the servant in the modern hotel who will drive
you mad with his constant demands for bakshish; the unveiled woman with a long modest skirt and headscarf who
walks arm-in-arm with another under whose *chadhuri** lurks

* The all-enveloping *chadhuri* makes a woman look like a walking
beachtent or a child playing ghosts with the bed linen. Such, at least,
it appears to one male eye. For a technical description, I am grateful to
be able to quote that of the wife of the Minister of the Interior. 'It is a
garment that has a cap which is usually very intricately embroidered,
and from this fall yards and yards of material minutely pleated, like
umbrella pleating in a skirt. Then in front of the face there is an embroidered section like a net, the embroidery so worked that the holes
are large enough for the wearer to see through. Then there is a heavily
embroidered piece falling down to the waist. The whole garment has
such a wide skirt that it can be pulled around the wearer so that no
part of her can be seen except her feet as she walks.' One might think
the garment, though cumbrous, is apt to keep out dust and heat; I am
told this is not so. (The garment is also called *burqa*.)

D

a hemline so truncated as to make the London fashions of 1966 look prudish; a serious midnight discussion between two drivers near the Persian border as to whether one should still drive on the left or change to the right; even the music is an amalgam of Eastern rhythm and Western melody.

Amid so many conflicting elements, to what zero does one turn a mental pointer? Where can one find a point of orientation from which to seek for coherence among such sharp contradictions?

Nowhere is the need to abandon preconceptions greater than in analysing the role of the Russians, erectors of the petrol pumps demanding the return to zero. We have already seen that, in the nineteenth century, their approach was unequivocally imperialist. Afghanistan represented to them a geophysical segment lying between Russia and its goal on the Indian Ocean: an objective to be taken as the southern khanates had been. Unfortunately, from the Russian viewpoint, Britain's empire was strong enough to make such an advance impracticable. Yet when, in 1947, the British obstacle was removed from the line of march southward to the shores of the Indian subcontinent, Afghanistan, stubbornly neutral, remained unmolested. Nor can this be entirely ascribed to Russian fears of a possible American riposte to the occupation of Afghanistan. After all, the United States felt unable to intervene in either Tibet or Hungary. But Russia must, on the other hand, have taken account of a firm American reaction to the second of the two inter-related moves, the one against West Pakistan with which, however, tenuously, America is still in military alliance. We should rather look for an explanation in the fact that, in this part of the world in particular, the dimensions of diplomacy and the expressions of power politics have changed.

*

Just as the great nineteenth-century improvements in transport by sea and rail altered the character of empires in Asia, Russian and British, so the twentieth-century revolutions in air transport and road-building techniques have changed the forms of great power predominance. The huge mountain range of the Hindu Kush, formerly so daunting to traverse as to demand full physical control of its high passes, no longer presents such a formidable barrier to the movement of men and goods. It is no longer a major political and military watershed. This change has coincided with the growing recognition in Afghanistan that better communications between the separate parts of the country are essential to its unity, to economic development and to the successful exercise of authority from Kabul. The Russians have been quick to capitalise on this recognition with offers of help in the development of civil and military aviation and of road building. The field has been largely left open to them, for Britain has renounced its imperial interests in the area, and the United States—only just beginning, and with some hesitation, to fill the power vacuum in Pakistan and, to a lesser extent, in India—plays a much less significant role in Afghanistan.

Nineteenth-century British strategists, concerned to keep Afghanistan an impenetrable buffer state, often warned grimly against the construction of a road south from Herat to Kandahar, for this would outflank the Hindu Kush. Today, you can drive in five or six hours between these two cities on a Russian-built concrete highway, striking boldly across the brick-red desert. Babur, the great Mogul, once struggled to stay alive in the deadly cold of a pass in the Hindu Kush by crouching in the corpse of an eviscerated camel. Now all the year round you can drive through the heart of these formidable mountains along the Russian-built pass and tunnel of Salang, or fly over them in the aircraft of Aeroflot—and at prices considerably below those of the international commercial airlines.

A glance at Map 2 (pages x–xi) will show that the only good roads in Afghanistan are those which are part of the system projected under the Second Five Year Plan. This system, completed in 1966, is shaped like the Russian letter Ц. Its lines of communication run from the Russian border north of Herat, through the major towns of Afghanistan (with the base of the

Ц thoughtfully provided by the Americans) and back to the Russian border at the Oxus port of Qizil Qala. The tail of the Ц runs down to the Khyber, where there is access—via Peshawar and Karachi—to the sea. A transit-trade agreement between Afghanistan and Pakistan was in negotiation at the time of writing that would allow Russian goods, if not Russian guns, to roll unimpeded down to the Indian Ocean 'in fulfilment of historic destiny'.

This triumph for Soviet diplomacy tends to be overlooked in the West. In terms of that economic competition which is the corollary—often ignored in the West but never by the Russians—of peaceful co-existence, access to a warm-water port within easy reach of the seaboards of Africa and South Asia, and through which its goods can be strategically despatched, is even more important to the Soviet Union than it was to tsarist Russia. Once the route is opened, the Russians will have an even greater interest than had the government of British India in the stability of Afghanistan and in friendly relations across the Durand Line.

But if the material evidence of the Russian presence is inescapable, in personal terms it is as discreet as ever, and sometimes it exhibits an almost psychotic sensitivity to the presence of curious Western visitors in Afghanistan. When I first visited Herat in 1957, what presumably were the first Russian survey parties had just begun their operations. Early every morning they paraded in their dungarees and boy scout hats, clutching their regulation brown attaché cases. Every evening they gathered in the garden to bemoan their exile and count off the days to home leave. When asked what they were doing, they would rather embarrassedly reply, 'We're on holiday'. Photographed, they leaped up in fist-shaking protest to have me detained by the Afghan police who, they seemed confident, would confiscate my pictures.* Today, their work is largely finished but they are still sensitive, particularly in the border areas. The visitor to Qizil Qala,

* Which they did most apologetically, only I had taken the precaution of switching films and so was able to publish the embarrassing evidence on my return to Britain.

however eminent the authority for his visit, will suddenly find at his elbow, within moments of entering the dock area, a large blond Russian who claims to be—and probably is—a maintenance engineer, but whose only discernible function seems to be maintenance of a close watch on the visitor until safely out of the gate. All along the far bank of the Oxus there are squat gantry-legged observation posts. The visitor with a camera who stands for more than a moment on the Afghan bank may find himself the centre of a diplomatic protest sparked off by a telephone call before his return to Kabul. Although no one seemed to object to my taking photographs at Ay Khanum on the junction of the Oxus and Kochak rivers, this area—site of one of the great archaeological discoveries of modern times—is still very difficult to visit.*

Even so, the Russian attitude has changed to some extent. If the Soviet expert in Kabul still walks discreetly in his drably coloured clothes through the market, in the provinces he is likely to prove eagerly talkative and open. An engineer in charge of installing cotton machinery chats and argues enthusiastically with the West Germans, Czechs and Afghans also engaged on the project. His chief—indeed, apparently his only—concern is that the machines should be got working

* The Hellenic site of Ay Khanum is remarkable almost as much for the way it was discovered as for what it contains. The King of Afghanistan, an ardent huntsman and a keen student of his country's history, was out hunting one day in 1963 along the Kochak river where it joins the Oxus. He came upon two unusual stones protruding from the ground: a Corinthian capital and an altar. He made no delay in getting these to the museum at Kunduz and in drawing them to the attention of the head of the French archaeological expedition, Dr Schlumberger. The early excavations conducted by the new head of the mission, M. Paul Bernard, have revealed at Ay Khanum the first complete Hellenic city east of Mesopotamia. Ay Khanum was probably built in the second or third centuries BC in the wake of Alexander the Great's conquest. The city and its hilltop fortress occupy a commanding strategic position with strong natural defences. There is evidence both *in situ* and in documentary sources to suggest that it was probably sacked and burnt to the ground towards the end of the second century BC by a tribe of nomads, the Urchi, from higher up the Oxus. Excited interest in the site, however, has to contend with 'difficulties' in reaching it. The author went there without asking; this, luckily, avoided the 'difficulties'.

according to schedule and that the Afghans become competent in operating them. A group of young Russian technicians at a textile factory seem more concerned in their free time to play what they called 'American' billiards in the company's club than to proselytise or read Marx and Engels. Some of the political pressure on the Russians has been taken off with their diplomatic success in Afghanistan; and sufficient mistakes have been made, enough machines have broken down, to have dispelled their early, and burdensome, reputation for infallibility. They have won much of what they wanted and so can relax a little.

Paradoxically, the very success of the Soviet Union's economic and diplomatic penetration of Afghanistan has arguably rendered its influence in that area much less harmful to the West. It would be a great mistake to go on using the terminology and assuming the psychology of a 'Great Game' which no one is any longer playing. In a sense, it has already been played and lost, with Red to move and nothing to prevent mate in two. Yet in the context of Russia's changing role in this part of Asia, the game has become relatively unimportant. Since the Tashkent Conference of January 1966 on the Kashmir dispute, Russia, as mediator between India and Pakistan, is very successfully playing the role of disinterested friend in the Indian subcontinent, with a weather-eye cocked over the high Pamirs. China's foothold on its frontier with Afghanistan is very small, but Peking's overall ambitions along the Himalayas and the mountain ranges which extend from them are a crucial challenge to Soviet foreign policy. But here is one area in which the contrast between what the Russians like to present as reasonable co-existence communism and China's 'militant', 'poor nations' communism favours Russia, for Chinese 'militancy' has all too recently been equated with aggression against its poor neighbours. Thus, only India's enemy Pakistan can readily be wooed towards the Chinese camp. (It would be a wry irony if ever China and America found themselves owning to a common interest in support of Pakistan against Russian ambitions!)

Red to Mate?

The Russian recognition that power-conflicts, economic in motivation, are now best conducted in purely economic terms, has had its effects on Soviet policy in Afghanistan as elsewhere. The Russians know that the rouble, cleverly deployed, is as good a weapon as the Red Army. In Afghanistan they have deployed it to good effect; and perhaps, in terms of their more immediate objectives, they have already conquered with it.

It is, of course, arguable that, if one interprets peaceful co-existence as the six-ounce economic gloves on the hard fists of ideological combat, then Russia's access to a warm-water port, however obtained, is a severe body blow to its opponents. Were this leather-padded assault backed by the killer instinct of ideological fervour, it might be construed as no less damaging than a bare-knuckled military occupation. Every day, however, Isaac Deutscher's theory of the 'embourgeoisement' of the Soviet Union, with the consequent dwindling of the killer instinct, seems to have more evidence to support it. In the Afghan context, it seems fair to evaluate Russian diplomatic and economic success as less harmful to a highly competitive West than the open challenge of physical occupation.

*

Afghanistan, more than most underdeveloped countries, depends on foreign aid for its development capital. In 1964–65, this latter amounted to 5,000 million afghanis.* Almost

* Monetary figures generally will be quoted in afghanis. To get the 'feel' of their real value, the reader should note that, though the official exchange rate is 200 afghanis to the £ and 71 to the $, on the black market in Kabul—which gives a better guide to real values than the official rates—in 1966 £1 would fetch between 210 and 220 afghanis and $1 between 75 and 78. In these terms, capital investment in Afghanistan is running at about £23 million a year. The standard of living is such that, in terms of internal purchasing power, this sum is greater; for example, a good three-course meal in one of Kabul's best hotels will cost between 45 and 60 afghanis (4 to 5 shillings). At the same time, it must be borne in mind that all industrial and technical equipment must be purchased abroad. The fact that Russia gives artificially favourable exchange rates is a further strengthening of the Soviet economic

two-thirds of the development capital in the current Five Year Plan comes from outside sources. In 1964–65, the foreign aid figure amounted to 3,400 million afghanis, made up as follows: 58 per cent from Russia, 29·7 per cent from America, 8·6 per cent from West Germany, 3·7 per cent from Britain and other countries. If to the Soviet contribution to capital development are added the advantages of trading with Russia —favourable exchange rates, low handling charges, no duties, the convenience of only having to transport goods to the Afghan border ports on the Oxus—it is clear that the bargain with the Russians is not only highly advantageous to Afghanistan but the only one of major importance. The outcome of all this, however, is that more and more of the country's economic life breathes only by grace of the Russians. Sad piles of old and discarded British cotton machinery can be seen outside a factory in the north, their place within taken by the latest Russian models. Admittedly, the difficulty of getting spare parts for Russian and other Eastern bloc equipment diminishes its appeal, and new British, West German and American machines are certainly being used to assist the slow growth of the country's industry. American equipment built the Kandahar–Kabul road. The British Bedford Company has signed a contract to supply trucks. Even so, the Russian predominance over Afghanistan's road communications is indisputable. In general terms, the overall picture is one of overwhelming and increasing dependence on Russian sources of supply.

In terms of personnel (other than diplomatic), it is very difficult to gauge how many Russians, with Czechs and other East Europeans, are at work in Afghanistan. The figure is probably in the neighbourhood of 2,000, as against 400 Americans and a dozen Englishmen. There is still such a

presence in Afghanistan. The capital investment figure quoted in the text was given to the author by the Minister of Finance and included a guess for the contribution of the private sector for which no accurate figures are available. Calculations of capital investment in the public sector based on IMF figures make it 4,193 million afghanis. (For a relation of wages to purchasing power, see page 75 below.)

shortage of qualified Afghans that, though usually in theory acting in an advisory capacity only, the Russian, European or American technician has in practice to do much of the work himself. The sudden withdrawal of these foreign technicians would have a crippling, if not a paralysing, effect on the economic life of the country. Afghanistan's leaders cannot be unaware of the consequences to China's development programme of the withdrawal of Soviet technical personnel and economic assistance in 1960. China made shift in the end to get over this heavy blow; Afghanistan without extensive outside help probably could not.

Dependence on Russia is even more complete in the Afghan armed services (about 80,000 strong), which are now exclusively equipped by the Soviet Union: well-equipped, indeed, albeit never with the very latest arms.* The airforce (with modern jet fighters) depends for spares and fuel on Russian supplies. Since care is taken by the Russians to ensure that there is never more than ten to fourteen days' supply of aviation fuel in the country, the Afghan airforce could be effectively grounded within a fortnight of a Soviet decision to turn off the tap. The majority of the younger officers in the armed services are Russian-trained, though it is necessary to add that, so far, there is little evidence in conversation with them or in the view of shrewd military observers to suggest that they have been politically influenced by communist doctrine or pro-Russian propaganda in the course of their training.

The Afghan economy, then, is heavily in pawn to its Soviet neighbour. Yet this is not a situation that seems in the least to perturb Afghanistan's leaders. Their imperturbability is probably justified. They are convinced that the Russians will not cut off aid since it is the price they are ready to pay for Afghan neutrality and for access to the Indian Ocean: a price which avoids incurring physical occupation of the route. The government in Kabul knows also that, as long as the Soviet

---

* It has proved impossible to get a precise breakdown of the Afghan armed forces. There is reputed to be one full armoured division, and the airforce is said to have two squadrons of MIG 17s.

Union sets itself up as the challenger to Chinese irredentist claims in Asia, it cannot afford even to be suspected of similar designs. Probably even more important in determniing the official attitude to Russia's economic predominance are the pride and self-confidence of the Afghan people, the vast majority of whom seem to be quite ready to be even poorer again if this should prove to be the price of independence. Nor are the Afghan authorities naïve; indeed, they can be rated as among the most expert takers of aid in the Third World. Though mainly in hock to the Russians, they have not allowed the bell of the Western pawnshop to grow rusty with disuse. And any remonstrance to them, suggesting that it is unwise to be so dependent on Russia, will meet the retort: 'Very well; then why don't other countries help us to the same extent?'

This is not to imply that they do not get aid from elsewhere. The Americans, as always, are making generous contributions to the economy. As indicated above, this is running at about half the Russian level; and it is, moreover, being administered much more wisely than in the past. There are some 200 people connected with the US aid programme in Afghanistan (housed palatially on the outskirts of Kabul), and an additional 200 unskilled Peace Corps workers.

The Americans have been considerably handicapped by their inescapable commitment to a single project in the Helmand Valley, inherited from the days when private American capital and know-how were being employed there by the Afghans whose original idea it was. In the early 1950s, the high-walled compound of the Morrison Knudsen Company seemed to be symbolic of the shuttered attitude of its employees. The Helmand Valley project was certainly imaginative in conception, aiming as it did to restore fertility to a vast desert area south-west of Kandahar and to revive something of Afghanistan's claim to its ancient title of 'the granary of Central Asia'. But a number of snags, particularly the salinity of the irrigated area, meant that more and more capital had to be sent chasing the initial investment. Happily however, the difficulties for this joint Afghan–American venture seem now to have been largely overcome. The closely-knit complex of irrigation and hydroelectric projects, with the ancillary social developments which are doing so much to pioneer advances in such fields as education and women's emancipation, can now be regarded as a notable success. Today, the United States is trying to diversify its aid programmes, and is particularly contributing in the fields of education, engineering and agriculture. There are four American teaching teams in Kabul University, and a teacher-training project, while Afghans are being trained in road construction, engineering and irrigation.

In agriculture, the Americans are breaking new ground in the development of wheat-growing in the north, at Mazar-i-Sharif, where some 300 new kinds of wheat have been tested. It is interesting in this context to note that neither Russia nor the United States, each with powerful domestic lobbies, is prepared to help Afghanistan in the cultivation of its most important cash crop, cotton—although, once grown, they are happy to help with processing it, and the Russians also buy some of the first stage products. (There is, however, a three-man British team engaged in advising the Afghans on cotton cultivation.)

United States aid administrators seem not unduly worried by Russia's greater role in the Afghan economy. Indeed, one of the most remarkable features of the situation in Afghanistan is that America seems content to accept the country's neutrality, even if this entails an economic bias towards the Soviet Union. It would be going too far to say that there is a 'dialogue' between the Soviet Union and the United States in Afghanistan, but certainly Russo-American relations locally have taken a turn for the better since the day in 1956 that the Russians cannily erected a grain silo outside Kabul in which to store the large quantities of American wheat sent under Public Law 480, and thereby gained credit among many Afghans for what was America's generosity. Perhaps a better symbol today would be the bridge at Dilaram—Heart's Ease—where the Russian-built road runs over the bridge put up ten years ago by an American engineer.

Afghanistan

The Afghans are almost certainly aware that it will greatly increase the volume of aid if they can keep Russia and America trying to outbid each other, or rather to keep the Americans at least within striking distance of the Russian total. It will be a nice exercise in diplomacy to see if the Afghans can keep the Americans sufficiently worried by the prospect of Russian domination of their economy to be generous but not frightened.

Afghanistan also gets help from other countries. After Russia and America, next in the aid league comes West Germany which provides, among other things, professors (who are unpopular) for the University of Kabul, and a forestry project (very successful) in the province of Paktya in the south-east corner of the country. Britain labours under the disadvantages of the legacy from the past, and until recently was not only powerless but without influence in Afghanistan. Until three years ago, any Afghan who wanted to visit the British embassy had to get police permission. As if resigned to this situation, the Foreign Office looked on Kabul as the last mission before retirement for diplomats past their peak. Then, in 1962, a young and vigorous ambassador was given Kabul as his first mission. Arthur de la Mare transformed the scene so much that Britain today, although its role is still small in Afghan affairs, is at least looked on as a country whose friendship is worth having. This Anglo-Afghan friendship finds material expression in a sugar factory at Baghlan and in the installation of new machinery for the extraction of seed-oil in northern Afghanistan. The British still approach the giving of aid to Afghanistan with a prudent measure of caution and with an insistence on economic viability. They hesitated, for example, to provide new cotton-gin machinery in Kandahar because of justifiable doubts about Afghanistan's ability to increase its production of raw cotton sufficiently to supply all the machines that have been, or are being, installed throughout the country.

Relations with neighbouring Persia are not so much bad as non-existent. The lack of ties between the two countries is brought forcibly home to the overland traveller between them.

Red to Mate?

The converging lines of rocks and pot holes—one cannot honestly call them roads—which lead up to the border are clearly intended to discourage rather than facilitate traffic (though plans are said to be in hand to rectify this), and the same is true of the customs posts and visa formalities on either side of the border. This lack of liaison and trade is particularly surprising in the light of the extensive cultural and historical heritage the two countries have in common. But Afghanistan is determinedly neutral and Persia a member of Western-orientated alliances and development plans; Afghanistan falls within the Russian sphere of influence, Persia just within the American. Nor is there yet complete agreement on exact topographical locations on every mile of their common, desolate frontier. So the two countries go their separate ways. Yet, in the long run, the strong, almost hereditary, cultural pull of Persia will probably draw them closer.

All the various efforts of the countries aiding Afghanistan, however, have to be set against the scale of the Russian contribution. They are all clearly outweighed by the Soviet aid programme, and the influence of these other countries is correspondingly less than Russia's. It may not be agreeable, but it is certainly inevitable, that Russia in the mid-twentieth century should have become the predominant power in Afghanistan: a country which Soviet forces could swiftly defeat and occupy if they wished. (Although it is doubtful if, in such an event, the Soviet Union would be any more successful than previous conquerors in controlling the Afghan people.) Not that Russia has, at present, any motive or desire for conquest. There are very cogent reasons why Moscow is prepared to pay a high price for an independent, stable and increasingly prosperous Afghanistan. Russia's interest in and investment for stability with its neighbour might not unfairly be compared with that of the United States in Latin America. Shrewd statesmen in the West may properly find some satisfaction in the fact that, in this part of the world at least, the Soviet Union is taking a share, without too many obvious strings attached, in the task of helping the underdeveloped world.

4

'Pushtunistan Unjast'

AFGHANISTAN UNJAST, Pushtunistan Unjast! Afghanistan Unjast, Pushtunistan Unjast! Hour after hour the shrill, monotonous cry of the lorry-driver's *bacha** drove one slowly to the verge of frenzy on the long journey, a decade ago, on the road from Kandahar to Kabul. 'This is Afghanistan, this is Pushtunistan!' It was as if a tourist on a motorcoach-drive down the Wye Valley from Monmouth to Chepstow were to find himself the captive audience of a fanatical Welsh Nationalist driver continually crying out 'Home rule for Wales, Monmouthshire is Welsh!'

The Afghan slogan draws its inspiration from the Solomon-like arbitration of the colonial boundary draftsmen. In 1893, the British government in India, in an attempt to persuade the Amir of Afghanistan to restrain his Pathan subjects from their periodic descents on Her Majesty's subjects in her North-West Frontier provinces, decided to establish a boundary commission to demarcate the frontiers between the Amir's and the Queen's dominions. After all, one could scarcely ask the Amir to restrain his subjects if he was uncertain as to who they were officially. Accordingly, Sir Mortimer Durand and his commission painstakingly delineated a frontier of military convenience, much of it running through the foothills which lead up to the Sulaiman mountains of Afghanistan itself. This 'convenient' frontier sliced through many tribal areas

* One of these agile youths, whose prehensile powers are quite amazing, is to be found clinging to the back of every Afghan lorry. His chief function is to leap perilously between the wheels whenever the vehicle stops on a slope and to thrust behind them the large wooden wedge that does service for the long-defunct brakes. He also helps the driver to collect the fares from the passengers. It is a kind of working apprenticeship.

50

with an apparently bland disregard for ethnic affinities. This
was matched by the steady disregard for British cartographical distinctions on the part of the people living along
what came to be known as the Durand Line; they crossed
from one side of it to another as if it did not exist, and were
naturally indignant, in the usual forceful Pathan way, whenever they met with reprisals or obstructions for so doing.
The restriction of an artificial frontier proved particularly
irksome for nomads whose lives and movements were dictated
by the location of traditional pastures from which they were
now sometimes cut off.

While Amir Abdurrahman, being a realist and bowing to
superior force, accepted the Durand Line frontier, he did so
grudgingly, for he was also a great patriotic leader and
regarded all the Pathan areas as properly a part of his kingdom. The determination to regain these districts is a strong
thread running through all subsequent Afghan history, and
the opinion that they form a natural part of Afghanistan is
strongly endorsed by Afghanistan's present rulers.

Lacking the relative strength which is the necessary ingredient of irredentism in the present climate of international
opinion, Afghanistan has over the years modified its demand
for the restoration of the old territory of the Durrani kingdom,
superficially at least, to one for 'Pushtunistan': an independent state for the Pushtu-speaking peoples south and east
of the Durand Line on the Pakistan side, Pushtu being the
language of the Pathan tribesmen of both sides of this
frontier. Such a state would naturally be expected to align
itself closely with Afghanistan, but would not be a part of it.
In the imagination of the Afghan cartographers, at least, this
has already been accomplished, for the tourist guides issued
to visitors clearly mark Pakistan's tribal territories as
'Pushtunistan'. What Afghanistan claims as Pushtunistan
corresponds to the North-West Frontier provinces of British
India, the boundary of which ran from the border with China
in the north to Baluchistan. (This latter area, it should be
noted, is not included in the proposed Pushtunistan.) It
traverses every kind of scenery, from the great mountains

and beautiful green valleys of Gilgit and Chitral to the Baluch desert—the dump, it is said, where Allah shot the rubbish of creation.

*

It is no marvel that this frontier should have been the setting of so many adventure stories of fifty or so years ago. Nature has conspired to create a backcloth appropriate to the character of the area's inhabitants. The scenic variety of the frontier districts on both sides of the Durand Line, indeed, seems almost unlimited. If you leave Kabul by the Lataband Pass as evening approaches, spiralling up the sinuous yellow road to 9,000 feet, you see the valley below and the hills around beginning to turn to a hard blue as the light fades. Then, as if nature is playing on a theatre organ, the sky's colour changes minute by minute. Just before the last streaks of purple, red and gold on the horizon darken into blackness, a storm breaks. There is no rain, and for a long time no thunder, and the lightning leaps nimbly from cloud to cloud showing up the mountains like a huge cardboard cutout. Here nature is so conscious of her power she disdains to bluster and threaten, and is content to dazzle. As you drive down the far side in the dark, the lightning projects a flickering photographic exhibition of small *chai khanas** revealed to their very depths, the lightning flashes so bright that the glowing lanterns on their verandahs are extinguished to the sight. Hills, trees and shrubs leap into momentary life, faces blink for a second and are shut in darkness again. Moving on down the Khyber at dawn to Peshawar, you leave behind the narrow defile speckled with innumerable plaques commemorating the otherwise forgotten deeds of heroism of those who fought to take and hold the pass.

Turning around at neatly geometrical, Raj-redolent Peshawar, your road leads south and west again, this time on the

* *Chai khanas* are the tea-houses which, in non-alcoholic Afghanistan, are the nearest equivalent to the Englishman's pub—or, rather, to the Irishman's or the Covent Garden porter's pubs, which are open pretty well all the time.

Pakistan side of the frontier, until you reach Kohat where a local restaurateur pounces to lead you to the heart of the town. You are being conducted to the sanctum of a master magician, past the booths of lesser conjurors and quacks— only the magic on this occasion is solely culinary. Don't close your eyes in passing each stall or you may succumb to the temptation of their many smells: roasting corn cobs, nuts and a variety of meats. With your eyes open the temptation will not seduce you, for their living coat of bulge-headed flies is enough to deter all but a starving or a Pathan stomach. The magician's cave itself is plunged in gloom, and against this background the long-bearded patron crouches over a row of gleaming bowls that catch the light prying through the open side of the shop. Raised on his dais, he deigns to give you a welcoming nod then, prince of devils, returns to gloat over and stir the vegetable afrits in his explosive cauldrons. A strong smell of spice hangs over them as they cook, although 'cook' is a tame word to describe the process, for gouts of yellow liquid leap like shell splashes round the bright red tomatoes which eddy round lower in the bowl, while rich green chilis, newly added, slip furtively between them.

Continuing your journey beyond Kohat, you are treated to a geological extravaganza. The road plunges into a crazy, Neapolitan ice of clay and red and yellow sandstone. The whole terrain has in many places been tilted through ninety degrees by the earth's movement, and yet the different strata are still sharply defined. Much of the softer layers has been worn away, leaving sharp fins of harder rock only a few feet thick but miles long and hundreds of feet high. The space between is occasionally cultivated, but more often it is just a bare hot strip of dust. From there you come to a region of harder rocks cut with gorges and passes, the road clinging to the lip of a ravine hundreds of feet above a marble-green river. Out of one pillar of rock a huge head, a hybrid of Greek and Asiatic, has been carved. From time to time you emerge from the gullies through the hills on to stretches of flat desert, or semi-desert, gravel and small stones, often crossed by wide, shallow watercourses left by the year's rain, which seems to fall in a wasteful few days and swiftly disappear. At one point, the desert is broken by an incongruous ten-mile belt of cultivated jungle, after which it changes its nature yet again. The scenery is startlingly evocative of one of Hollywood's fanciful films about the Foreign Legion. The desert, with its outcrops of honeycombed sandstone, high temperature and Colorado atmosphere, is dotted with 'legion' forts, manned by the North-West Frontier Force. The desert is the home of a multitude of dust demons: spirals of sand thirty to a hundred feet high which swirl tortuously across the landscape, elastically changing shape as they go.

You may spend the night at one of the garrisons where the officers' mess seems more Sandhurst than Sandhurst but where the entertainment is essentially Pathan: a display perhaps of tribal dancing and satire. The dance is rather like the Afghan *atan*, the dancers hopping about like birds and jerking their heads sharply from side to side, thus making a flying plumage of their long black hair. The music is without melody, the rhythm varying greatly, the dancers coming at moments almost to a standstill and at others jumping and stamping in a sforzando of frenzy punctuated by regular crashing breaks. The musicians, four in number, walk slowly round inside the circle of dancers, clapping on small tabors or playing on a wailing reed instrument. The purpose of the dance is to excite a battle frenzy; erotic dances, common to Western cultures, play but a small part in these predominantly male societies. By the glazed look of some of the dancers after forty minutes, the desired result seems to be achieved. The dance is followed by a pantomime which gives full scope to the Pathan's great gift for mimicry and comic gesture, and in which the ordinary soldier seizes the opportunity to satirise his officers.

The journey gets harder as you drive on south-west, this time in the cab of a bus bursting at the rivets with passengers; there are twelve in the driver's cab alone. The floor is heaped up with baskets; jammed tightly against them, you prop your feet on a stone water-jar, knees pushed up to the chin so that you can scarcely move in any direction and are forced

into the meditative position of a more than usually maso-
chistic fakir. Your clothes stick in clammy swabs to those
of your neighbours and mutual sweats mingle in one steady
flow. On one side of you is a man with 'flu and on the other
his pock-faced son who leans his head on your shoulder and
sprawls over your legs. A third, clad in a loud check shirt is
jabbering and spitting like a human monkey, and all over
you crawl two small children whose lips and faces are burst
open by suppurating boils and festering sores. The heat,
sweat, noise and stench is such that even the acrid smell of
biri, the rolled tobacco leaves that make up a Pakistani
cigarette, is a welcome anaesthetic.

At last you reach Dalbandin, the town everyone has been
talking about in the bus. You feel an immense relief, but when
you clamber out you realise that Dalbandin is only a small
group of huts around a few government offices, a fort and a
railway station: a mere village surviving in a wilderness of
sand that assaults it in tireless waves which appear to be
sucking up its outposts inch by inch. Yet there is a gaunt
beauty in its few blasted trees waving desperate, crazy fingers
out of their graves of sand and in the simplicity of its white-
fronted buildings defying the desert. On one edge of the
village, next to the football pitch—just a patch of sand a
little less soft than the rest—you find a resthouse that has
somehow snatched a comparative paradise from the ground
of this desert hell. There is a pool in the compound, and grass,
and green trees, and clumps of a lovely bush which blossoms
with warm pink and orange flowers.

On again, this time in the single-track train that runs like
a lifeline through the Pakistan frontier provinces and Baluchistan. You are now out of the territories of the Pathans proper
and well into Baluchistan. Here

> The desert singes, and the stubborn rock
> Split to the centre sweats at every pore.[1]

Your nostrils are suddenly assailed by the pungent odour of
the earth's flesh on fire, scorching beneath the sun as un-
mistakably as that of any human body. For over two hundred

miles there is no water at all except that brought once a week in the wagons of the train. Nor is there any natural wild life except the 'sandfish': a small snake-like creature about the size of a blindworm and of a light sandy colour. There is nothing apparently for it to live on, yet it survives, and from its tail the natives extract a precious oil used in the making of perfume. Villages here exist only because of the treasures of the desert and the black hot hills that traverse it: manganese and other minerals or, as at Nok Kundi, the most beautiful marble in Asia. Perfume and marble; Eve's beauty from the serpent's tail and palaces quarried and fetched from the very mouth of hell.

★

It is these varied territories and differing peoples of the southern frontier districts which the Afghan government dreams of making into a single coherent state. The lorry-driver's *bacha* should be calling, not *Pushtunistan Unjast,* but *Pushtunistan Kujast?*—'Where is Pushtunistan?'

Apart from the sentimental attachments of the royal family, a mixture of gratitude and fear probably provides a subconscious motive for the desire of Afghanistan's auto-cratic monarchs over the past thirty years to see the Pathan areas as a whole come within a greater degree of Afghan control, however theoretically indirect. During the chaos that followed Amanullah's overthrow in 1929, the British carefully refrained from any involvement and, verbally at least, tried to disassociate the tribesmen on their side of the frontier from the subsequent struggle for power in Afghanistan. These British admonitions, however, were ineffective, and the bulk of the tribal forces which gave Nadir Shah, the present King's father, the ultimate victory were, in fact, recruited south of the Durand Line. Even if today the spontaneous reaction of the tribes would not by itself be sufficient to overthrow any Afghan régime which had the backing of the army, it is still a powerful factor in the country's politics, and one of which any ruler, democratic or autocratic, has to take account.

Whether the Pathan tribes south of the border still take

much interest in Afghan affairs is very open to doubt. Since 1947, the Pakistan government has made great efforts to make these tribes feel that they belong to Pakistan and that their citizenship brings substantial material benefit. As a deliberate act of policy, expenditure in the tribal areas on education, health and rural development has been disproportionately high in relation to expenditure on these things in other parts of Pakistan. Conversely, the transfer from tribal law and customs to the rule of national law has been tactfully gradual. A steady recruitment of men from the tribal areas to the Pakistan regular army—among whose élite troops such North-West Frontier forces as the Waziristan Scouts stand supreme—also serves to increase their attachment to Pakistan. When they are released from military service to return to their villages, they take with them not only the skills and literacy but the attitudes that they have acquired in the army. It is perhaps significant that in many villages it is regarded as a matter of honour to furnish the local quota of men for military service.

The division of the Pathan tribes by the Durand Line led, after the partition of the Indian subcontinent in 1947, to an uneasy relationship between Afghanistan and Pakistan. The Afghans felt that their ambitions were now opposed by a weaker force; the Pakistanis, acutely conscious of their problems in welding together a new state from so many disparate entities, were determined that nothing should detract from strengthening the sense of national unity. Inevitably the two countries came to loggerheads over Pushtunistan. The dispute has fluctuated in intensity for twenty years, at times quiescent, at others—as in 1960–61—on the brink of outright war. This clash in 1960–61 is worth examining a little more closely, for it marked a turning-point in their relations.

Diplomatic relations between Afghanistan and Pakistan had been resumed in 1957 after a two-year lapse following the merger of all the Western States of Pakistan, including the North-West Frontier province, into a single West Pakistan. But, at the end of 1959, Pakistan felt compelled to protest against violations of its air space by Afghan aircraft and against provocative broadcasts on Kabul radio by the King and Premier in which both, in the name of Pushtunistan, repeated earlier claims to parts of Pakistan. These incidents were the culmination of a persistent and increasingly tough attitude fostered by Prince Daud, then Premier (and a cousin of the King) over the Pushtunistan question. In March 1960, Khrushchev publicly supported the Afghan claims. Pakistan riposted by proposing a referendum among Afghan Pathans to see if they would like to join Pakistan. The Afghans retorted by refusing to extend the visas of Pakistanis working in their country, expelling a number of them and making the life of those who remained virtually impossible. Pro-Pushtunistan propaganda was intensified by Afghan consular agencies, whose activities in this field had already aroused deep indignation in Pakistan.

It is difficult to decide exactly who started the fighting which broke out in the Bajaur area, north of the Khyber Pass, in September 1960 and again in May 1961. Pakistan claimed that it was repulsing incursions into its territory by armed groups backed by the Afghan army. The Afghans counter-claimed that Pakistan was in fact conducting a severe campaign of military reprisals and bombing against discontented Pathan tribesmen within its own borders. The Pakistanis admitted the bombing of one house, which they said was the headquarters of Afghan agents. Apportioning blame in an area where the movements of population are considerable is not easy, although personally I feel that Pakistan probably had slightly the better case. Whatever the origins of the conflict, diplomatic relations were broken off in September 1961 and frontier traffic came to a standstill. By November, something like 200,000 Afghan nomads, who habitually leave their summer pastures in Afghanistan for winter work in Pakistan, found themselves stranded and near starvation in the mountain passes between the two countries, although a few managed to force their way over the border. The closure of the frontier was a sharp blow to the Afghan economy, and its consequences contributed to the resignation in March

1963, after ten years as virtual ruler of Afghanistan, of Prince
Daud, who then held the position of Premier. He was replaced
by a commoner, Dr Mohammad Yusuf. Of uninfluential
origin, Yusuf was the first meritocrat in post-war Afghanistan
to reach the top by diligence and ability (he holds a Ph.D.
from Göttingen). With Daud gone, tension between the two
countries began to ease and, through the good offices of the
Shah of Persia, diplomatic relations were restored in May
1963. All the same, and granted that the Russian attitude has
been modified, the ingredients of the situation still exist. A
similar cycle of suspicion, protest and combat could all too
easily be set in motion again.

There is no doubt as to the strength of feeling aroused by
this issue. Muhammad Hashim Maiwandwal, the present
Prime Minister of Afghanistan, made it quite clear in conversation that he thinks the Pushtunistan issue is as serious
now as ever—perhaps even more serious than before in that,
despite the expressed regret of both sides over the clash in
1960–61, there has been complete failure to resolve the dispute
to the satisfaction of all three parties: Pakistan, Afghanistan
and the Pathans. It is necessary, therefore, to examine the
validity of Afghanistan's claim and the viability of any
proposed state of Pushtunistan.

*

The basis of the Afghan claim is that the Pushtu-speaking
peoples are an artificially divided ethnic entity. That they
are of the same race on both sides of the Durand Line cannot
be in dispute, but that this border is the artificial and sole
cause of division is open to argument. It is fallacious to
assume that the Pathans are a naturally homogeneous whole.
Their entire history is, rather, one of fierce and cruelly conducted intertribal disputes over everything from grazing
grounds to kingdoms. Great tribes like the Yusufzai and the
Durrani have been continually at skirmish with each other
for centuries, and feelings of deep antagonism remain.

The essential characteristic of the Pathan tribe is a closely
knit and sharply defined pattern of family relationships that

places everyone not of that group, and quite irrespective of his ethnic origins, among the world of potential enemies. At the same time, the Pathan—of whatever tribe—has a strong pride in being a Pathan. The tribal group is the limit of the extent to which the Pathan is prepared to abate his jealously guarded individualism. Even within the family circle, rivalries and quarrels are often long and bitter, since the Pathan calls no man lord and admits his inferiority to nobody. To the world outside his tribal group, and apart from the demands of hospitality to wayfaring strangers, the Pathan's attitude alternates between a total indifference and a kind of tigerish contempt for the rest of the human animal kingdom, whose function is to provide, when necessary, individuals to satisfy the predator's appetite. Mountstuart Elphinstone, a most penetrating observer of Afghan life, graphically describes the character of the Pathan in his *Account of the Kingdom of Caubul.*

> Their vices are revenge, envy, avarice, rapacity and obstinacy; on the other hand, they are fond of liberty, faithful to their friends, kind to their dependents, hospitable, brave, hardy, frugal, laborious and prudent; they are less disposed than the nations in their neighbourhood to falsehood, intrigue and deceit.[2]

The Pathan character has changed little since the year 1814 when Elphinstone completed his account. Gun-carrying is no longer mandatory, nor failure to go armed a case of being improperly dressed; but one man in four still carries rifle, shotgun or pistol, and those that no longer go gun in hand still have one at home—just in case. Gaily decorated, near-perfect handmade imitations of the classic weapons of every nation are manufactured at the tribal arms factory near Kohat in Pakistan; examples can be seen bristling from the top of every market-bound bus or lorry. The occasional ornate *jezail* (one of those ancient muskets which seem more likely to destroy their owners than their targets) or the intricately decorated sheath of a triangular-bladed hunting-knife evoke memories of the stirring adventures vividly narrated by writers of the

Henty school and hardly less vividly re-enacted by many a British schoolboy in his back garden.

Generosity and nobility of manner can yield to the most scathingly expressed form of contempt in the world: an ice-basilisk glance and a tiny gobbet of precision-planted spit at the despised one's feet. Moving with a springing stride, toes turned slightly inwards and rising at the heel, and with a tall, haughty carriage, the Pathan will flash at you from beneath stern black eyebrows a fierce look that can turn suddenly into a shy glance of soft brown eyes. Warlike spirit shares his soul with childish and delightful vanity, and a Pathan will lay down his rifle and cartridge belt, sit on a little peninsula of stones by the stream and pluck, paint and preen himself with more than a woman's vanity in the mirror-shine of the lid of a boot-polish tin. A courteous and unembarrassed 'good day' from him, striding past you as you attend to the call of nature in the desert; the care and protection of you, his guest, as an unquestioned obligation, even to death; his manly independence; his Rabelaisian humour—all this makes the Pathan a man to be liked and respected, to be treated tactfully and carefully; and a man rarely, if ever, to be organised within the impersonal conventions of a modern state.

It is highly unlikely that people of such a prickly and individualistic temperament, inheriting many intertribal enmities, antipathetic to the very idea of central rule, are going to agitate very forcefully for the creation of Push-tunistan—unless such agitation can serve as a means for satisfying their, at present, much thwarted lust for a good fight. Their outlook is, after all, little different now from the days when the Pushtu poet, Khushal Khan, trying vainly to unite the tribes against the Mogul Emperor Aurangzebe, bewailed: 'Would that the Pushtuns could agree among themselves.'

Nor can a good case be made for Afghan claims in inter-national law. Pakistan is the legal and indisputable inheritor of British power and British territory in this part of the world, and every British government since 1947 has clearly

61

recognised and stated that fact. Britain and Afghanistan, however unwillingly in the case of the latter, agreed by treaty on the frontier between them along the Durand Line; Afghanistan, therefore, cannot legally repudiate that agreement with Britain's successor, the government of Pakistan.

But the real weakness of Afghan claims, to those more concerned with justice than law, lies in their lack of logical coherence, their internal contradictions. During an amiable, lengthy and courteous interview with me, the Prime Minister for just one brief instant sparked a flash of anger; it was when I asked him whether he thought any part of Afghanistan should become part of Pushtunistan. His sharp 'never' and subsequent rebuke of my 'irrelevant' question betrayed, not only strength of feeling, but perhaps also an awareness of the ambiguity and weakness of the arguments for an independent Pushtunistan. If there is a case to be made out for Pushtunistan on the grounds of natural ethnic affinity, assessed in terms of language, then all Pushtu-speaking peoples, from both sides of the border, should belong to it; which means that it should be created from territories belonging to Afghanistan no less than to Pakistan. If this case falls, partial groupings cutting across established states and boundaries make no sense in terms of securing stable and equitable territorial demarcation in this part of Asia. It may, however, seem to make sense in terms of other considerations. It will be seen, when we come later to examine the attitude of the Pathan ruling group in Afghanistan towards the minorities there, that the assumption by this group that Afghanistan is already a natural Pathan state has at least as much, and may be more, significance for internal as for external interests.

One should not expect those involved to apply pure logic to the argument, in public at least. Pushtunistan, like the reunification of Germany, is one of those causes that no national leader or politician dare renounce, however little faith he may himself have in it; the cause has its own logic. Yet danger lies in an issue which, kept simmering for a variety of reasons, can suddenly come to the boil through some political accident. At one time, as has already been indicated,

there was certainly a grave risk that more intense heat would
be applied to the simmering pot by the Soviet Union. For
long it was an axiom of Russian policy that the Durand Line
was part of a wicked imperialist plot which it was Afghanistan's duty to overthrow. In August 1951, for example, an
article in *Literaturnaya Gazeta* declared:

> As a direct result of the enforced division of the Afghan
> tribes, who are almost equally divided between Afghanistan
> and Pakistan and are carrying on a struggle for self-
> determination, and also as a result of the original traditions
> of the numerous nomad tribes, a situation is arising
> apparently of itself, apparently spontaneously, in which
> there could occur demarcation by bloodshed of the frontier
> that was originally plotted on the maps of the imperialists
> in London and [*sic!*] Washington. Spontaneously rising
> tension, mutual enmity and incidents are exactly what the
> imperialists need in order to divide and rule.

It so happened that 'tension' and the rest were also exactly
what the Soviet imperialist philosophy of that time needed to
facilitate its territorial expansion. But since the clash of
1960–61 between Afghanistan and Pakistan, the Russian
attitude has changed. Having made a notable effort in 1965–66
to compose the quarrel between India and Pakistan over
Kashmir, Russia will not want to see yet another frontier war
flaring up in an area where the development of its interests
requires stability. Moscow now seems to recognise that such
divisions in the Indian subcontinent are of benefit only to
Peking. The main aim of the current Soviet diplomatic effort
seems to be to persuade Afghanistan and Pakistan that they
have mutual economic interests, for it is on their recognising
this that the unhampered outflow of Russian goods through
these countries largely depends.

The governments of Afghanistan and Pakistan are certainly
becoming more aware of their mutual interests; and in their
dealings with one another, if not in their public pronounce-
ments, 1963 seems to have marked the beginning of a new
phase in their relations. It is probably too early to say that

they are 'co-operating', but at least the current situation seems to be one of acceptable stalemate. Hard reality is imposing its restraints. Pakistan cannot afford further frontier involvements when already overextended in its struggle with India over Kashmir. Rumours that Indian diplomacy at the time of the Indo-Pakistan war in 1965 was seeking to embarrass Pakistan on the latter's north-western border may have been well founded. Not that Pakistan is likely to make concessions to Afghanistan; it cannot discuss claims on national territory, let alone relinquish part of it, while engaged in trying to make good its claims to Kashmir. For its part, Afghanistan now realises that it cannot afford to provoke Pakistan again into closing the common frontier, although this does not diminish its long term irredentist aspirations. Afghan leaders still cannot refrain from making just those claims on Pakistani territory which, if given any practical interpretation, would assuredly provoke something more than a 'closed frontier' reaction from Pakistan.

Pushtunistan is an issue which has appeared to be perpetually poised on the brink of disaster yet which has never actually toppled from its precarious ledge into open conflict. The chief hope that this delicate balance can be preserved lies in the fact that the Pathan tribes themselves seem, by and large, content with their respective national allegiances, and this the governments in Rawalpindi and Kabul know—even if they won't admit it.

5

Disunity and Cohesion

THOUGH OFTEN the most dramatic, relations with other states are not the most critical of Afghanistan's problems. The real tasks facing the government are internal: the problem of unity and minorities; the conflicting pressures, social and economic, of traditionalism and modernisation (particularly in regard to the status of women and to Islam); and the difficulties of imposing sophisticated political methods and institutions on old tribal loyalties and attitudes. In subsequent chapters, we shall examine political developments in Afghanistan in recent years and assess the country's economic resources and the attempts made to harness them. Here we shall trace the main features of Afghanistan as a society and seek to explain the factors that condition its political and economic development.

WHO ARE THE AFGHANS?
The most challenging of the problems facing Afghanistan is the creation of a sense of genuine national unity in a country whose constituent races have as little natural affinity as had those of Britain before and immediately after the Norman conquest. When most foreigners use the word 'Afghan', they are usually thinking of the Pathans, forgetting that among the country's inhabitants are very substantial minorities of Uzbegs, Hazaras, Turkmen and Tajiks, not to speak of many smaller groups.

While placing great verbal emphasis on the need for national unity, the government of Afghanistan does little to foster it in practice. Indeed, it seems to think that unity is something that will come of its own accord. The present Prime Minister optimistically declared during an interview: 'We do not think in terms of ethnic entities. We consider everybody in Afghanistan as Afghans.' This is an admirable goal at which to strive, but most of the minority groups would not agree with him that it is already achieved. They feel that Afghanistan is a country run by Pathans for Pathans and that the other groups are, in a sense, the victims of an internal colonialism. This is an impression which must be shared by the foreign visitor. It is strengthened by the government's preoccupation with exclusively Pathan issues, such as Pushtunistan, the status and use of Pushtu (see Constitution, Art. 35, Appendix IV), and the dominance of the 'Pathan' capital, Kabul.

Numerical comparisons are hard to make since there are no census returns or any other reliable population statistics, although an attempt to provide these will be made during the current Third Five Year Plan. The population probably amounts to between 10 and 15 million;* the upper figure is the more likely. Of these, approximately half are of Pathan origin. There are substantial minorities, estimated at about a million each, of Uzbegs, Hazaras and Tajiks, of which the Tajiks are the largest. The picture is further confused by the nomads, who may number at least 4 million and are drawn from various ethnic groups: Turkmen, Baluchi and so on, as well as Pathans.† A form of Persian known as Dari is the language common to these groups (not necessarily as the first language), except that many uneducated Pathans speak only Pushtu. The government of this volatile mixture is firmly in the hands of the Pathans. In a cabinet of sixteen members, there are only two non-Pathans. You will find Pathan governors in most of the provinces, even where the population is predominantly of another ethnic group, but not—partly, it is true, because of the problem of the Pushtu language—a non-

---

* D. N. Wilber (*Afghanistan*, p. 33) gives strong reasons for preferring the lower limit. He estimates the nomad population at 2 million.

† By far the largest and most important of these groups is the Ghilzai, the most numerous of the true Afghan tribes, and with a reputation among foreigners for fanaticism and savagery unequalled even in Afghanistan. At one time the Ghilzai (or Ghalji) conquered much of Persia.

Pathan governor of a Pathan province. The overwhelming majority of administrators are also Pathans. In fairness, it must be said that the Pathans have a flair for administration and that even in an openly competitive society, without ethnic bias, they would probably come out with more than their share, relative to their proportion of the population, of key government and administrative posts.

The favoured position of the Pathans in modern Afghanistan is symbolised by the way in which Kabul thrives, apparently at the expense of the provinces. In amenities and services, Kabul is fast becoming a typical modern metropolis. New blocks of offices and houses are springing up among the old mud dwellings; cars, restaurants and well-stocked shops abound, as one would expect in a capital city. But its array of amenities and services is out of all proportion when the city's 450,000 population is compared with that of the whole country.

For example, over half of Afghanistan's sorely needed 700 doctors practise in Kabul, where the prospects are best of augmenting their meagre government salaries by private practice, and where there are hospital facilities. This gives Kabul a ratio of one doctor per 1,300; but in Khwaja-i-Gar the doctor has 200,000 patients on his list, no hospital, no assistants, no nurses and not even a local dispensary for drugs. His is the only car in the district and he works for a salary of 2,000 afghanis (£10 or $28) a month with little chance of adding to it by private fees. Similarly with education; the capital has almost a monopoly of the best facilities. Almost all institutions of higher education, universities and technical colleges are at present centred in Kabul, although a start has been made in extending them to Jalalabad, Herat and Mazar and in expanding the technical college in Kandahar. A student who has once been to Kabul does everything in his power, or more often in his family's power, to avoid being sent back to the provinces. This is particularly true of the few women students. The provinces are thus deprived of the very people needed to demand and create the missing amenities and services, and so the vicious circle continues.

While it is true that members of other ethnic groups in Kabul do benefit from its growth, the capital is essentially a Pathan-dominated city, and its growing modernity is viewed with envy by the provincial Uzbeg or Hazara. As yet few of these are sufficiently educated to appreciate the extent of the imbalance and to turn their resentment into any more active protest.

On the other hand, improvements are also taking place in the provinces, and it is these which present the immediate picture to the less sophisticated. To draw on the medical example again: the province of Samangan, in the north, now has four doctors and a small hospital catering for sixteen patients, together with an effective malaria control campaign, whereas ten years ago it had absolutely nothing in the way of medical services. But even provincial development is concentrated in the Pathan areas to the south and south-east of the Hindu Kush. The great schemes of agricultural development in Khost and the Helmand Valley, of forestry at Ali Khel, of hydroelectric power and agricultural irrigation in Nangarhar—these are all in Pathan provinces; and even where development is taking place in regions where other groups predominate, as with cotton ginning and processing in the north, at Kunduz and along the Oxus, it is often in an area with a Pathan settler population dating from the government's deliberate shifting of Pathans to these areas before the Second World War.

In the main, the Pathans live south of the great barrier of the Hindu Kush, and the bulk of the minority groups live to its north or in the south-west. Until the Salang Tunnel was opened in 1964, the mountains to all intents and purposes, in winter at least, sealed off one half of the country from the other. Over the last few years, communications between Kabul and the main provincial cities have improved considerably, both by road and air, although such important centres as Mazar-i-Sharif and Gardez are still linked to the capital by dirt roads whose monstrous potholes and fist-sized stones prove the best free breaker's yard in the world for any car. Communications between the provinces themselves

are virtually non-existent. To travel between Mazar-i-Sharif
and Kunduz—the capital of the important neighbouring
province of that name—you take your choice of the various
tyre-tracks across the desert of those who have passed before,
and at the same time try to follow the meandering line of
dilapidated wooden beanposts bearing the single telephone
line. To reach Kunduz you must cross the river by a wooden
ferry whose ballast system, a masterpiece of ingenious
simplicity, consists of baling water from one of the two hulls,
side by side catamaran style, to its equally rickety partner,
while motive power is achieved by hauling on a rope. The
180-kilometre journey between the two towns takes nine or
ten hours' driving, with time off for digging two-wheel-drive
vehicles out of the sand. There is not likely to be more than
a single vehicle travelling in the opposite direction—which
in these narrow switchback tracks is just as well.

But these appalling communications must be seen in per-
spective. Compared with those of ten years ago, they are a
tremendous improvement. Whereas then the 900 miles from
Herat to Kabul could take ten days on the back of a lorry,
it can now be done by car in not much more than ten hours,
and military road-building teams are hacking good roads out
of mere narrow tracks in provinces like Paktya. In terms of
immediate traffic there is perhaps no great need for very good
provincial roads in a country where the bulk of transport is
still by camel and donkey, horse and bullock cart, and where
even great baulks of cedar wood find their way to Pakistan,
two or four at a time, strapped to the sides of a camel. Yet in
terms of creating a sense of national unity and of promoting
co-operation between the different provinces and groups, the
establishment of good communications from province to
province, as distinct from the direct links with Kabul which
are a permanent reminder of provincial dependent status, is
essential. The difficulties and expense of such a road-building
programme should not be underestimated. These roads would
have to cross deserts of shifting sand and stark black granite
outcrops, go over rivers whose spring floods can wash away
a solid stone bridge in a few minutes, and pierce mountains

which climb to 18,000 feet. It may be that the prospect of a low-cost steel industry (see chapter 7) indicates that railways —lacking in Afghanistan today—are the best long-term investment, while for the immediate future aircraft, and perhaps hovercraft, might provide the answer. None of these alternatives is cheap, but money spent on fostering a sense of unity is a sound investment, even if it brings in its wake still greater pressures from the provinces for a larger share of the national expenditure.

★

The present imbalance in favour of the Pathans, and the official preoccupation with Pathan nationalism, can only serve to alienate the minorities completely. This is particularly true of the Uzbegs: a sophisticated and capable people who provide the bulk of the country's professional men and entrepreneurs. The amount of private capital reinvested in the national economy is still, so far as it is measurable, pitifully small. The Uzbeg entrepreneur often feels no confidence in Afghanistan and its economy as a whole, feels he has no stake in the country and therefore often prefers to keep his surplus wealth in the local equivalent of a sock under the mattress. Such men have to be persuaded to invest in the economy by being given practical proof that they will have a reasonable say in its overall direction. Desperately short of capital resources, Afghanistan cannot afford to neglect internal private wealth. The development of industries associated with the discovery of natural gas at Shiberghan, right in the heart of the Uzbeg country near Mazar-i-Sharif, offers splendid opportunity for Uzbeg entrepreneurs to identify private with national interests. This, however, will be baulked unless there is a marked change of line in Kabul. If excessive emphasis is placed on ethnic affinities, and if it is legitimate in official circles for Pathan ambitions and interests to be projected southwards over the Pakistan border, then it can hardly be less legitimate for the Afghan Uzbegs to turn their eyes northwards across the Oxus to Russian Uzbekistan, where all their cultural affinities lie and whence, indeed, they derive their racial origins. One has only to witness their almost magical performance on horseback in their sport of *buzkashi* (which combines mounted mayhem with rugby football played with a beheaded goat) to realise that, in ethnic terms at least, their ties are with the horsemen of Soviet Central Asia.

In the early days of post-war economic penetration, the Russians were not slow to exploit this affinity by the extensive use of Russian Uzbegs in development projects in the relevant areas of Afghanistan; and, of course, those with radios are within reach of the ordinary domestic broadcasts of Soviet Uzbekistan. Clearly, any feeling of divided loyalties among such a powerful and capable minority would be fatal to hopes of Afghan unity; but it should be remembered that, while the sociologist, anthropologist and historian may look to the wider picture, the ordinary Uzbeg—for the present at least and despite the increasing influence of radio—is far more concerned with his immediate neighbours.

The Hazaras, whose Mongoloid features and truculence of manner, betray their descent from the hordes of Genghis Khan,* do not require the support of outside influences to strengthen their intransigence. Living in the central mountain area known as the Hazarajat (an extension of the Hindu Kush), they are almost literally inaccessible to all forms of central government or authority, from tax collection to police. The extent of their isolation can be judged by the discovery only a few years ago of a large, beautiful and historically important minaret near Jam; and the traveller trying to reach it may still enquire in vain at a village less than ten miles away. The isolation of the Hazaras is further aggravated by the fact that they alone of any major group of Afghans belong to the Shi'a sect of Islam, and are consequently despised by their Sunni fellow citizens. There are practically no employment possibilities in the Hazarajat; and this, since the area is largely barren, aggravates the discontent of the Hazaras. Official talk of a road linking Herat and Kabul through this area is still largely wishful thinking, but

* The exact nature of this descent is much disputed by ethnologists, but that the Hazaras are of Mongol origin is not in question.

the discovery of large and very high-grade iron ore deposits at Hajigak near Bamian may in due course go some way to solve the employment problem and so bring the Hazaras within the conventional pattern of a modern state.

Of the principal minority groups, only the Tajiks are unlikely actively to oppose any signs of Pathan colonialism. They are, by tradition and inclination, a peaceful people—poets, dreamers, intellectuals—who earn their living by farming in the regions round Kabul, Kandahar and Herat. They are proud of being Tajik in an unassertive way* and have a quiet and tactful courtesy towards strangers. Their attributes, like those of the other minorities, could be valuable ingredients in the emergence of the new Afghan nation for, if nations have characters, then there is no doubt that a balanced combination of the virtues, and even vices, of these four races could produce an impressive character indeed.

Across all these groupings, like a restless and repetitive air plucked on the metal-stringed *rebab*, runs the life of the nomads. Those dust clouds on the horizon, when you come closer, are seen to be living acres of sheep and goats, or a long line of camels piled high with tents and utensils with mother and child perched atop, for once enjoying a rarely experienced ease. The women, in their rich greens, veil themselves a little at the sight of strangers, although purdah is not their domestic practice since it inhibits their role as the family workers. The camels, gaily decked out with bridles of fine blue, white and red beads, are preceded at a jaunty trot by the dogs. Boys and men, each with a stout stick, ride their fine horses or walk round their flocks, for the dogs seem to have little herding skill. Soon they merge into the yellow haze again on their way to the high cool pastures of Badakshan. These are the nomads of the north. In the south, donkeys are perhaps more common than camels, rifles than knobbly sticks, women on foot than those riding. The colours are brighter and more varied, the column a little less orderly. North and south, the countryside is dotted with the nomads' flat tents which stand out like

* It should not be forgotten, however, that they, like the Uzbegs, have links across the Oxus with their kindred in the Soviet Union.

black blisters on the hot red flesh of the desert or merge into
the background of dark hills; or perhaps they live in the round
and carefully decorated felt huts of the more permanent settle-
ments into whose shadowy recesses the women disappear
behind growling dogs at the first glimpse of a camera-bearing
stranger.

It is not only on the frontiers with Pakistan that these
nomads present problems. Since they are highly suspicious
of any attempt to record their numbers or movements, for
fear of making themselves more liable to government interfer-
ence and control, such positive developments as education,
medical services, agricultural improvement and parliamentary
representation are rendered largely ineffectual in their case.
They feel little loyalty to such an abstract concept as the
state of Afghanistan or to its fixed symbol of power, the
Kabul-centred government. There is, in addition, a fierce
rivalry of long standing between the Ghilzai (Ghalji) and the
ruling Durrani tribes.

*

It is difficult to believe that the government can be unaware
just how strong are the fissiparous tendencies in present-day
Afghanistan. These became dramatically evident during the
student riots of October 1965, which were largely instrumental in bringing the present government to power. A very
shrewd American observer told me that the students naïvely
believed that armed police, mostly Uzbegs and Hazaras,
would not be brutal to them or fire on demonstrating fellow
countrymen, albeit Pathans. In fact, my informant told me,
the police—simple country lads for the most part—revelled
in the chance to 'have a go' at the city-slickers from the
Pathan capital of Kabul. Two of the students and one by-
stander were shot dead in the ensuing fracas.

The problem facing the government is an intractable one,
for it is precisely those Pathan characteristics making for
efficient exercise of authority that also make unity among the
different races difficult to obtain. There can be little amity
and sense of common purpose when one race feels itself

73

innately superior to the others, whom it considers as irremedi-
ably second-class citizens. However, this attitude probably
holds good only in a primitive agricultural and tribal society.
The rapid modernisation, industrialisation and urbanisation
of Afghanistan may to a considerable extent undermine this
structure of freemen and helots. But this will only be the
case if the government realises (and so far it shows little sign
of doing so) that, for unity to become a reality, it must be
created by positive action favouring the minority races with
a distribution of resources which is proportionate, not to their
actual numbers in comparison with the Pathans, but to the
leeway that has to be made up and to the need to identify
them as equal partners in the national life of Afghanistan.

CLASS, WEALTH AND WOMEN

The great contrasts between wealth and poverty common to
most underdeveloped countries are scarcely evident in
Afghanistan. This is because even the middle and upper
classes, or the majority of individuals among them, are
relatively poor and because outlets for conspicuous consump-
tion are few. Buildings, carpets, flocks and land and, in the
north, the superb *buzkashi* horses on which a man will gladly
spend a small fortune—these are almost the only investments
for accumulated wealth. There is still virtually no private
industrial and commercial large-scale investment, and the
commodities on which, in a consumer economy, the rich
spend their wealth are very hard to obtain in Afghanistan,
due to lack of foreign exchange. Indeed, it is quite likely that
the nomad families with the largest herds are among the
richest people in Afghanistan, although their wealth cannot
really be converted to measurable terms.

Yet, if evidence of the heights of wealth is scarce, it is
equally rare in Afghanistan to come across any stark display
of the depths of poverty which are so harrowing in more
densely populated, if richer, underdeveloped countries. The
children, boys and girls, are generally well cared for and fed,
and are almost extravagantly well clothed. The signs of

disease are plentiful, but the emaciated limbs and swollen stomachs of severe malnutrition are rare. There is some begging, but not the persistent buzzing swarm of importunate human flies common to other Eastern countries. It is not easy, either, to tell rich from poor, or at least from relatively poor, by outward appearances. Their style of dress and diet is much the same, and their houses, although different in scale, are usually similar in external appearance and design. In Kabul, it is true, distinctions are beginning to emerge, but only because the capital is ceasing in many ways to be typically Afghan and is acquiring some of the depressingly identical cosmopolitan features of all capital cities.

Income per head is probably only a little over 4,000 afghanis (£20 or $56) a year. Basic wages, with little opportunity for overtime, for an Afghan industrial worker are from 600 to 1,000 afghanis a month. To buy himself a good meal, the lower paid Afghan works for about four hours; for a pair of slippers, six hours; and for a telephone call, four minutes.* To buy himself a new Land-Rover, which carries a 130 per cent sales tax, he would have to work for nearly a hundred years. The professional man, or even the cabinet minister, is only a little better off in terms of income. As we have seen, a doctor may earn only 2,000 afghanis a month or even less, while a cabinet minister has a salary of only 10,000 afghanis a month. The Prime Minister himself receives but 25,000 afghanis a month. It is true that the more enterprising merchants and big landowners can make substantial incomes, but there are not many in this class.

When every Pathan is a prince in his own eyes, and men of other races are strong in personal pride, it is not easy for the

---

* In fact, it is highly unlikely that he would be able to make one. Although a telephone call costs only about a farthing, there are at present in Kabul no more than 6,000 automatic telephones. By the end of the Second Five Year Plan (March 1967), it is envisaged that this number will have been increased to 15,000. Although telephone communications throughout the provinces are being improved, and the old rickety single lines are being replaced by double and even quadruple lines firmly strung across metal posts, it can still take several days to make telephone contact between one provincial centre and another.

casual observer to detect local equivalents of those class differences that abound, with all their social minutiae, in Western societies. Evidence of a racial hierarchy we have already noted; the hierarchies within each community are much harder to detect. Where these exist, they tend to be expressed in the form of official positions in the administrative and government structure, for government activity embraces a far wider spectrum of activity than it does in Britain, for example. These positions in turn frequently depend on nepotism (it is thus pleasantly surprising to meet the Finance Minister's nephew doctoring in one of the remotest provinces) and on the extremely complex patterns of family relationships and rivalries, of which the blood feud has only been the most dramatic expression.

The art of family power politics depends largely upon the ability to marry off the women of the family in such a judicious way as to keep its wealth intact, and for the men to marry in such a way as to increase the family fortunes. The ramifications that these marriages have led to over the generations are almost impossible for the stranger to follow. In effect, however, for the 'class' distinctions of Western society one can substitute the word 'family', if one is seeking out special divisions and barriers. The privileged members of Afghan society come from no more than a dozen or so families, but 'family' has to be interpreted very widely to include degrees of cousinship which would scarcely be traceable in Western society. Even so, it can fairly be said that Afghanistan does not suffer from those two divisive plagues of Western society: class antagonism and wealth snobbery.

*

The most strikingly obvious divisions in Afghanistan are between the sexes. 'Eve span and Adam dozed' might be the proverb here, for while the men sit around chatting in the *chai khanas*, the women do much of the day-to-day work, not only of the house, but of the field. This inequality is enshrined in the system of purdah: a conception which, incidentally, is quite alien to the pristine tenets of Islam.

Purdah is not merely the wearing of the all-enveloping *chadhuri*; this sartorial isolation only symbolises the whole position of women in Afghan society as inferior beings set apart, automotive chattels. The setting apart of women extends to every aspect of life: their rooms, their meals, their upbringing. Even in their love life their status as amatory partner is usually regarded as inferior to that of the male, whose universal jealousy can often be so extreme as to make poor Othello seem like a complacent cuckold. A love affair is as likely to involve another man or boy as a woman. Many of the poems of the great Pushtu poet, Khushal Khan, are unequivocally and unashamedly written to youths.

Purdah is basically an urban phenomenon, less stringently practised and enforced in the villages, and by the nomads scarcely at all. Its extension and retention are at least partly the fault of the women themselves, in the view of one shrewd lady (a foreigner married for many years to a very prominent Afghan). The *chadhuri* was seen as a social status symbol and the poorer women, particularly peasants moving into towns, would obtain one as soon as they possibly could in order to imitate their city sisters whom they regarded as their social superiors. Certainly, the *chadhuri* is a great equaliser among women since it gives the ugly ones a chance. But, women being what they are, differences in the material and workmanship, and the air of wearing it by one passing purdahed woman as against another, are soon apparent.

Afghan women have been officially quite free to dispense with the *chadhuri* since 1959 when, in a pronouncement to this effect, Prince Daud—so often belittled as an arch-conservative*—began the tactfully gradual introduction of female emancipation. Soon the brave among the more prominent women were showing the way and others followed suit. Yet, even today, as you walk round Kabul you will see fully half the women still wearing the *chadhuri*. If you travel

* 'Arch-conservative', we should add, in domestic affairs only. By the Americans, at least, he was no less exaggeratedly dubbed 'the Red Premier' because of the extent to which he invoked Russian economic aid.

in the provinces, you will scarcely find half a dozen women who will go without it in public. In the bigger provincial towns women, even foreign visitors, will sometimes attract contemptuous comment from the male bystanders if they are unveiled. Remonstrance that the unveiled one is only following royal precept leaves them unmoved, for the Afghan man is no fool and sees the immediate implications of the disappearance of purdah for his own easy way of life. Unfortunately, few of them have yet seen that, in the long run, purdah can only hamper the growth of their prosperity.

Purdah in Afghanistan is based on the concept of a woman as a man's property. The governor of one district (Chahardarra in the province of Kunduz) explained to me with some pride the way in which the region's beautiful hand-woven carpets were made; how five or six women might work together for four or five months to make a patterned carpet, 9 feet by 6 feet, for which they would get 1,600 afghanis,* and how a man would pay a very good bride-price for a girl who was an accomplished carpet weaver. When I asked him who got the money for the carpets, he looked at me in astonishment and replied: 'Why the man of course, the woman belongs to the man.' It is this attitude which is the chief obstacle facing the champions of women's emancipation in Afghanistan.

Those who dislike the idea of feminine equality, but do not wish to oppose it outright, adopt many subtle arguments. They ask why there is any need for emancipation when Afghan women already wield so much power within the family. After all, it is the women who arrange the all-important marriages on which the family fortunes may depend, and it is often the oldest woman in the family to whom all its members hand over their earnings and wealth for her to manage and augment. She it is who in many cases holds the family purse-strings. But these are subtle sophistries, for such power is exercised only on sufferance or by strength of will, not as a recognised right. In fact, it is this very

* The carpet would sell at nearly twice this price in the bazaar at Kabul, and four or five times as much by the time it reached a European or American drawing room.

family structure which helps to perpetuate the inferior role of women. The value of a marriage arrangement often depends on the fact that a woman has no property rights in marriage, and that property, therefore, reverts to the male side of the family when a woman dies—contrary as this is to the *Shari'at.*

Under the old customs, it was virtually impossible for a girl to refuse to marry the man of her parents' choice, for the marriage was seen as an important property transaction, one not to be thwarted by mere personal whim. Moreover, the parents could invoke the law to support them in any conflict with an erring daughter who decided she did not fancy her betrothed. Today, however, although most marriages are still arranged—and are not necessarily the less happy for that— the girl's wishes are normally consulted and no penalty is exacted for refusing to comply with the parental will. More matches are made, too, on the initiative of the man and woman themselves, for love. The shy pride of a doctor or a teacher who tells you he married for love is something new on the Afghan scene.

There are two major weapons in the Afghan emancipator's armoury: education and economic opportunity. Through the first they can encourage the women to rebel against their inferior status, through the second to rebel successfully. It is significant that practically all the leading women in Afghan public life who are fighting for a better deal for their sex have been teachers of one kind or another, and are concentrating their efforts on creating wider educational opportunities for girls. These, at present, are very limited. In the province of Paktya, for example, the military administration has set up forty-one primary schools for boys, but there is only one for girls and this was started by two officers' wives. In Kunduz, the governor is looked on as a daring progressive (as in this context he is) because he has set up, not only a new girls' primary school—the mischievous, curious manner of whose pupils belies the demure outward appearance of black dresses and white headscarves—but also an adult education institute for women where such subjects as home management are taught. He also has women working—with women patients,

of course—in the hospital. In another province, the governor
is trying to start secretarial courses for girls like those in Kabul
(where the first successful lady-typists are now to be seen in
government offices and agencies).

Women have just begun to break through into the pro-
fessions. There are sixty women doctors, and now the Minister
of Health is a woman and very respectfully referred to as 'Her
Excellency' by the men doctors who work for her. There is
even a very good woman engineer. Women nurses, health
visitors and malaria control officers are coming forward in
increasing numbers. But here the problem is always the same:
to get them to go out into the provinces and the villages where
their influence is most desperately needed. Husbands and
brothers still generally refuse to let a woman in medical work
stay away from home overnight. (Treatment at second hand,
where the doctor is a man and the patient a woman, is still
practised in many areas; the husband or father relays questions from the doctor, symptoms from the patient and
treatment back from the doctor, without doctor and patient
ever meeting face to face.) Life is not easy for the woman
who goes to the provinces and the counter-attractions of
Kabul are very strong: not only the amenities and services,
and the better health of her children, but the fact that in
Kabul she is one of many women tasting freedom. In the
provinces she will often be a lonely and conspicuous pioneer.
If she wants to further her education, her chance of doing so
in the provinces is very small. The provision of such opportunity is thus a critical point in changing women's traditional
role in Afghanistan.

Yet education, without economic opportunity, is not
enough. If she is to have the courage to assert her right to live
her own life, a woman must be able to feel confident that she
can defy her family and social pressures and taboos, and yet
still make her own living independently. She will also want to
appear attractive out of purdah, to have good clothes, shoes
and make-up now that her form and features no longer lurk
behind the *chadhuri*—and this costs money. In law, an
Afghan woman is entitled to equal pay for equal work; in

practice (as is not unknown in more 'progressive' societies), she does not get it.

In the first place, there is very little work that a woman can take up outside the 'ministering' activities of medicine and education—air-hostessing must probably be counted as 'ministrative' too. The most important and rapidly expanding new field is secretarial work, for which, with the modernisation of Afghan industry and commerce, there is an increasing and unsatisfied demand. There are also a few women employed in manufacturing—as opposed to cottage—industry, particularly in the Spinzar Company's pottery works in Kunduz, and in some textile processes. But here, also, the inequalities are evident. Women pottery workers of four years' experience in doing the delicate trimming operations on the unfired teapots and jugs, for which most men's hands are too clumsy, earn between 500 and 600 afghanis a month. Although, in theory, the rule is equal pay, men doing similar —and, if anything, slightly less delicate—work further down the production line earn from 900 to 1,000 afghanis a month. Criticism of the Spinzar Company for this disparity has to be tempered by the recognition that it is a real pioneer in employing women at all. Credit must be given, too, for its ingenuity in starting this employment in a field where even the most censorious anti-feminist has to concede that women are guiltless of the crime of rivalling men, because men, in fact, are incapable of doing the work. In the country where sudden and sweeping reforms introduced by Amanullah came to such a disastrous end, it seems as if a gradual, pragmatic approach may be successful. These are certainly the tactics now being employed by the reformers.

The full rigours of purdah are normally imposed at the onset of puberty, a little before the age of twelve, when the great majority of Afghan girls leave school. The provision of further education and training institutions to bridge the gap between the school-leaving age and taking up relatively independent employment at, say, fifteen or sixteen is of critical importance, for it will enable the girls to evade the start of purdah. Once this has been accomplished, it is much easier for them to maintain their emancipated condition. The spearhead of the emancipation campaign is the girl in this category, supported by girls from enlightened families in which purdah is abolished. Manpower shortage in the unskilled categories is certainly not an Afghan problem at present. It remains true, however, that an underdeveloped country has little chance of making substantial progress unless it has freed the energies of its women so that these can be applied to national objectives.

A number of remarkable individual women, some of them foreigners, have campaigned for women's rights in Afghanistan over the past twenty years, but now the movement's most prominent leaders are the four women deputies elected to the Wolesi Jirgah, the lower house of the Shura (parliament), in the elections of October 1965. In these, women were both allowed to vote and to stand, although not many took advantage of their rights to do either. One of the women deputies for an area just outside Kandahar was certain that, in fact, not a single woman had supported her. (Her election was due to the last-minute withdrawal in her favour of the two male opponents.) The others were opposed by men; remarkable as it must seem, they were elected by a predominantly male electorate. These four women deputies— Mrs Mahsuma Wardaki, Mrs Rokyan Abu Bakr, Dr Anahita Ratebzada and Mrs Adija—have already made a considerable impact in parliament, showing themselves the equals of the best men deputies. Their influence has principally been exerted in the areas of special interest to them, such as education and women's welfare, but it is not confined to these. They readily admit the need for prospective women parliamentarians to acquire a wider general knowledge of politics, but it is clear from my conversation with them that their own political range is by no means narrow.

Putting their views on women's role in Afghanistan, Mrs Wardaki and Mrs Abu Bakr argued most cogently that the inferior position of women in Afghan society offends against both the constitution of the state and the religion of Islam. The constitution demands that laws and government should conform to the laws of Islam. The laws of Islam, the emancipators argue, protect the rights and status of women; hence, to the extent that the exploitation and domination of women is permitted in it, Afghanistan is an 'ungodly' state in which the tenets of Islam and their constitutional validity are being questioned.

It would need an expert in Islamic lore properly to appraise this 'liberal Muslim' argument. It is certainly arguable that there is less scriptural justification for the inferior status of women in the Koran than in the New Testament, where Saint Paul makes it very plain that wives should be in subjection to their husbands. Particularly striking is the way in which the Koran specifically mentions 'men' and 'women' separately rather than collectively in setting out such matters as rights to property and access to Paradise (e.g. *Surat al-Tauba*, v. 71 *et seq.*). On the other hand, there is the positive statement (*Surat al-Nisa*, v. 23) that 'the men are set over the women'— although theologians have expended much energy in arguing just what 'set over' means in this context. The sympathetic Westerner may well feel that, in the Afghan situation, these niceties of theological debate are less important than the fact that the women deputies have at least made a pre-emptive bid against those conservatives in the Shura who might oppose emancipatory reforms on the grounds that they were contrary to Islam.

The argument of the emancipators is certainly shrewd. However, it is not likely to carry much weight with the mullahs, the religious leaders, for these have come to epitomise in the name of Islam the conservative opposition to female emancipation.

ISLAM

'When these reforms come in, Islam will go out', declared one angry mullah and was promptly clapped in prison by Amir Amanullah, whose rash attempts to make Afghanistan a modern state overnight, with equality between the sexes, secularised education and democratic institutions, had provoked this declaration. But the mullah had the last laugh, for the rising inspired by his fellow mullahs succeeded in putting the clock back again, and in due course Amanullah lost his throne.

Today, these reforms are being reintroduced, more subtly, more effectively and in a more welcoming climate of public opinion. Is it still right to assume with the mullah that Islam and the progressive social development of a modern state are incompatible? If it is, what will the outcome of the conflict be? Now, as in the past, the role of the mullahs is critical. They, after all, are the interpreters of the Koran and of the Islamic faith to a simple people. If they claim that women's role is properly an inferior one, will it make any difference for militant females and liberal scholars to declare that such a conception is contrary to the true doctrines of Islam?

Islam has no ordained priesthood but rather a pastorate of knowledge—though it is permissible to refrain from adding 'and of wisdom', for often there is but little of it. The original thinker, particularly in Sunni Afghanistan, is looked on as a dangerous man, for the whole pattern of religious learning is based on a process of repetitive ingestion and regurgitation, generation after generation, of the same arguments and doctrines with no attempt to adapt them to changing circumstances. Such a dogmatic process of instruction, exercised on those generally drawn from the lower and peasant class, tends to lead to bigotry and narrow-mindedness, in things temporal as well as spiritual. Anything which falls outside the compass of recorded knowledge and has no precise precedent is, for the mullahs, either insignificant or inimical. It would be wrong to suggest that there are no good and wise men among the mullahs, but the significant point is that training and circumstances aggravate the limitations of the mediocre who are the great majority.

There is an awesome multitude of detailed rules for the conduct of private and civil life which has to be learned by the mullah, and such is the number and complexity of these rules that the ordinary citizen who wishes to conduct his life in accordance with Koran and Sunna has no option but to

seek the mullah's guidance. Indeed, the Muslim's word for
his priesthood, in the Sunni if not Shi'a persuasion, is *ulama*
or 'knowers'. The mullah has often been the only focus of
law and learning in many a village and small town. Since the
law is based on the Koran—and indeed the new constitution
also firmly lays down that this shall be so (Arts. 69 and 102)—
the mullah lays claim, not only to the authority which comes
with the power of moral and spiritual judgement and leadership, but also to the authority derived from his role as an
interpreter, however indirect, of the law governing the daily
lives of the villagers. Moreover, the *madrasah* system of education has for long given the mullah a position of authority
vis-à-vis the local people from childhood onward; in this
system, the mosque and the school are virtually synonymous,
and the method of learning applied is a miniature reflection
of the pattern of the mullah's own education. Until very
recently, this sterile form of rote-learning was the only one
available.

Up to the first generation of this century, when the
authority of the mullahs was at its most formidable, they had
it in their power to rouse the people to war with their cries of
'Islam in danger', and often did so. Religion was very much an
ingredient in the perennial border clashes with British India,
the Afghan War of Independence of 1919 and the revolutionary overthrow of the would-be reforming Amanullah in
1929. Even ten years ago, the authority of the mullah and
respect for him were virtually unquestioned in Afghanistan.
He could jab a clear space for himself with his umbrella in the
back of a dangerously overcrowded lorry without protest, and
the foreigner who forcefully objected was in danger of being
thrown off by the other passengers as an impudent *feringi*.
The mullahs are still the mainstay of the conservative opposition to reform, indeed to change of any kind. Often ignorant
and bigoted men, they are at least shrewd enough to realise
that reform can only mean the end of their almost exclusive
authority and a decline in their status.

Such a decline has, in fact, been taking place over the last
decade—so much so that the mullahs are no longer in a

position to veto all progress, provided changes are made gradually and tactfully. The main reason for this decline in influence is the growth of alternative sources for the authority and educational opportunity of which the mullahs once had a monopoly. Education, albeit still in very short supply, is available through state schools, where the tenets of Islam are certainly still taught, but learning them by heart is no longer the only mode of instruction. As the economic and political structure of the country becomes more complex, so the tentacles of administrative, secular authority reach out further and further into the rural areas. The law is becoming more a matter of police and lawyers, legislation, courts and judges; although still based on the Koran, it has an increasingly secular flavour, in which nice legal arguments about evidence have replaced precedented but inflexible interpretations of the Divine Will. The mullahs should not be under-rated; in sufficiently catastrophic circumstances they could doubtless strongly influence the destiny of Afghanistan; but they are not the power they were.

The decline in the influence of the mullahs does not necessarily imply any decline in the importance of the Islamic faith in Afghanistan. The seemingly inevitable divorce between religion and everyday life which accompanies the urbanisation and industrialisation of a simple rural society is only occasionally in evidence in Afghanistan. Belief in Islam and the practice of its rituals are still the almost invariable rule throughout the country. Admittedly, over an interval of ten years one notices the slight secularisation—if that is the right word—of some members of the upper and middle class. A bottle of Scotch will appear on the table and be drunk as willingly by the influential Muslim host as by his guest. A scientist will admit to scepticism; a government official will regret that he feels Islam an anachronism in the context of social progress. (This latter argument will sometimes meet with the riposte that a return to the original purity of Islamic doctrine would, in fact, be conducive to progress—as, for instance, in the case of the status of women.)

But these few, sceptics and reformers alike, are the exceptions. The great mass of the people accept and believe in Islam in exactly the form that their fathers have done for many generations, ever since their conversion at sword-point in the tenth century AD. There is no mistaking the way in which Islam has become a deep-rooted part of Afghan life. 'Please excuse me while I say my prayers', says your host, gesturing for you to continue drinking your tea while he turns away into a corner, thus fitting his religion naturally into his daily life. Or perhaps it is the touching simplicity of the nomad who walks a little apart from his flock and kneels on his prayer mat, his brown clothes and black *pugri* standing out starkly against the evening skyline, to say the prescribed prayers; or that same mullah who so uncharitably wielded his umbrella and who now climbs down from the lorry in some isolated clump of huts and under the single tree leads the villagers in prayer by lantern light.

For the Afghans, the observances of Islam are an integral part of life's daily routine. Yet the observances are perhaps more important to them than the faith. Sometimes you cannot help feeling that the gesture of the hands spread behind the ears is indicative of nothing so much as the worshippers' own deafness to the strident cries of a new world. The mosques are coolly beautiful. The pale blue and dark green glazed tiles, the simple curved architecture, the pleasantly laid-out gardens, have all the dark unhurried calm which befits a place of worship. Yet how far is it the quiet of decay rather than of tranquillity? I could not help feeling in Afghanistan (and must admit to knowing too little of Islam for anything but personal impressions) that the centuries-old faith had lost the capacity for change and would be left behind in the Middle Ages when every other aspect of national life had finally made its painful way into the twentieth century.

*

Other faiths are now tolerated in Afghanistan, and their practice, provided it gives no public offence, is protected by the new constitution (Art. 2, para. 2). In effect, however, this is largely a gesture to foreigners. Of the great faiths that were once universal in Afghanistan (like Buddhism) or had their origins there (like Zoroastrianism), there is scarcely a trace of either relic or practice today. Islam is perhaps a little more isolated in Afghanistan than it is in other Muslim countries. There is no truck with the Shi'a doctrines practised in neighbouring Persia; indeed, these are looked on by the strictly orthodox Sunni Afghans as effete and corrupt. This attitude is an additional factor in the antagonism between the Pathans and the Hazaras, the latter being Afghanistan's only major Shi'a group.* Nor does Afghanistan seem to make much of the brotherhood of Islamic nations, perhaps because its major source of international disagreement is with one of them.

Of that trio of tolerances so frequently invoked in human rights' charters—'without discrimination in regard to race, sex or creed'—the first two, in Afghanistan, may be divisive factors; but the third, the religion of Islam, is very definitely a unifying factor. It is the major cultural and spiritual common denominator of ethnic groups that otherwise have little is common. But, although it is a unifying factor which enables the government to relate laws and administration to an acceptable premise, understood, however dimly, by all the people, it is not, as some would wish, necessarily a barrier to the communism of its giant neighbour. The argument is that, being so strongly theistic, a Muslim country provides no vacuum for the materialistic doctrines of communism to occupy. Yet, in many respects, Islam itself is a materialistic faith, and the dogmatic nature of its belief may be in keeping with the dogmatic approach of communism. Perhaps Islam, in its rigid and materialistic forms, is sufficiently similar to certain features in communism for the one to open the way for the other. There is, however, a major factor which may hamper the spread of communism in Afghanistan: the fact that there Islam is the faith of a fiercely independent group of individualists. It is this individualism that is likely to provide the antithesis to communism rather than religious doctrine as such.

* There are also some very small Pathan tribal groups that are Shi'a, but most of these live on the Pakistan side of the border.

Disunity and Cohesion

There is, in fact, very little indication of communist influence in Afghanistan today, and the real assurance against the growth of such influence in the future is the rapid development of a form of democracy which both gives expression to Afghan individualism and also enables the government to function efficiently. This is precisely what the leaders of Afghanistan are now trying to create.

6

An Experiment in Democracy

*We, Muhammad Zahir Shah, the King of Afghanistan, in the name
of Almighty God, do herewith sign the new constitution of Afghanistan
approved by the Loya Jirgah in its session in Kabul beginning on the
18th and ending on the 28th day of Sumbullah, 1343. We promulgate
this new constitution today throughout the entire State.*

THE 'TODAY' of this proclamation was October 1, 1964:
a day marking the beginning of a remarkable experiment in
democracy, the success of which is by no means certain but is
important beyond the bounds of Afghanistan itself. Muhammad Zahir Shah was deliberately abandoning two hundred
years of autocratic rule and diminishing his own personal
power in order to give his country a system of government
which would survive, as an absolute monarchy could not, the
stress of the twentieth century.

THE NEW CONSTITUTION

The new constitution,* proclaimed in 1964 and to come into
operation a year later following Afghanistan's first elections,
imposes some surprising and shrewd restraints on the exercise
of power. In particular, it bars the royal family from both
politics and government (Art. 24, para. 5), thus imposing on
the recently ousted Prince Daud perpetual exile from the
corridors of power and closing the backdoor of quasi-
constitutional usurpation to any possibly dissident relatives.
It also sets up a representative system of government formed
by the Shura (parliament) consisting of the directly elected
Wolesi Jirgah (House of the People) and the partly elected
and partly appointed Meshrano Jirgah (House of the Elders).
The older institution of the Loya Jirgah (Great Council) is

* See Appendix IV, page 147 below.

now composed of members of both houses of the Shura and the chairmen of elected provincial councils. The Loya Jirgah's functions are partly formal and partly to act as the sounding board of national opinion in times of great stress, such as a royal abdication or a state of emergency.

In promulgating this new constitution, the King seemed to be deliberately effacing himself and minimising his power. His Majesty Muhammad Zahir Shah is an exquisitely well-mannered, highly civilised man, more interested in the culture and history of his country and in open-air sports than in the practice of government and the exercise of power.* He has a very real love of his country, and wisdom enough to know that the absolute authority of his family would ultimately be an obstacle to Afghanistan's progress.

Yet it would be a grave mistake to look on the new constitution as a total abdication of the royal authority. Certainly, it imposes conditions and restraints: the King must be an Afghan national and, in effect, of the House of Nadir Shah; he must be a Muslim and a follower of the 'Hanafi doctrine' (Art. 8). But he also retains extensive reserve powers. Among royal prerogatives are the dissolution and summoning of the Shura (Art. 9, paras 3–6), the appointment of the Prime Minister and other ministers (Art. 9, para. 11) and of the Chief Justice and senior civil and military officials (Art. 9, paras 13 and 14), and the proclamation of a state of emergency (Art. 9, para. 16). It is true that the King must govern within the limits of the constitution, but that same constitution insists that 'the King is not accountable and shall be respected by all' (Art. 15).

The restrictions on the political role of members of the royal family have to be seen in the context of Afghan history, in which the most likely suspects in any plot against the King's life were his nearest, though not necessarily his dearest. It is less than fifty years since a younger son outplayed and outfought his elder brother for the succession; less than forty

* This opinion is based on hearsay only for, despite protracted and tantalisingly hopeful negotiations, I was unable to obtain an audience of His Majesty, although promised one.

years since an Afghan monarch, Nadir Shah himself—so frequently styled 'martyr' in the new constitution—was assassinated. The constitution's caution is no more than realism demands. The problem of the succession is always a delicate one in an autocratic system, whether the autocracy be regal or 'proletarian'. It is at the death of the ruler that the state is most prone to upheaval and to the chaos that accompanies any prolonged struggle for power among aspiring heirs. The new Afghan constitution goes into considerable detail in setting out the line of succession in the royal house and the conduct of any necessary regency. Particularly significant is the provision by which no one who has acted as permanent regent can subsequently become king himself (Art. 28, para. 5).

Nor should one quibble at the powers still reserved to the monarch. After all, the monarch in the United Kingdom still has in theory very considerable powers, and the fact that they are exercised on advice and not by the Crown's 'mere motion' is the outcome of custom and practice over a long period of political stability. It is not unreasonable to suppose that in Afghanistan, given a sufficient period of stability, the power of the monarch could similarly become more of a ritual than a reality. Much depends on the personalities of the next two or three monarchs; and here again we must note the bearing of the constitution's provisions regarding the role of the royal family in politics and its determination of the mode of the succession.

The critical factor in the evolution of democracy in Afghanistan, given self-restraint by the monarch and members of the royal house, will be the extent to which government is derived from the popular will and is answerable to more than the personal whims of its members.

*

The Wolesi Jirgah is directly elected every four years by the universal suffrage of all Afghans over the age of twenty. (We shall see later how the first of these elections was conducted.) It consists of 215 members representing single-member constituencies and elected by the single-direct-vote system as practised, for example, in Britain. The Wolesi Jirgah could, therefore, become as truly representative as any parliament elected by this rather crude method can ever be. Of the 84 members of the Meshrano Jirgah, one third are directly elected every four years from constituencies coextensive with the 29 provinces, one third are representatives elected every three years by provincial councils to which they have previously been directly elected, and one third are members appointed every five years by the King 'from amongst well-informed and experienced persons' (Art. 45, para. 1). Thus, the composition of both houses of the Shura, and of the Loya Jirgah as well, is predominantly democratic, with members answerable to the voters at regular intervals.

The division between legislature and executive is absolute; and it is perhaps in the way that this separation is organised that there lies the principal weakness of the new constitution. The Prime Minister is appointed directly by the King and then recommends a list of ministers to him. Neither the Premier nor other ministers may be members of either house of parliament, and should they be so they must resign their seats on appointment to office.* The Premier then submits his government to the Wolesi Jirgah for approval, first outlining its general policies to the lower house. The Wolesi Jirgah has the power to grant or withhold its vote of confidence, and it is the lower house alone that has this power of veto. Only when the government receives a vote of confidence does the King issue the necessary royal decree of appointment.

The Premier, however, has no machinery of party whips through which to exact that vote of confidence (the organised

* A striking feature of the constitution is that members of parliament, ministers and judges are expressly forbidden to follow other occupations (agriculture and 'free enterprises' excepted) during their terms of office (Arts. 52, 87, and 99 para. 3). Free enterprise, while a vague phrase, has so far been interpreted to mean land and property ownership. The Minister of Mines and Industries, for example, would not be permitted to run an agency for one of the international petrol companies. Conversely, no judge, civil servant, military officer or member of the government may stand for parliament while still holding office (Art. 47).

party as understood in the West being still unknown in Afghanistan), and battle has already been joined on the interpretation of Art. 89 of the constitution in so far as it affects the membership of the government. The fall of the first government to hold power after the elections of October 1965 and its replacement by the present administration demonstrate that the battle for ultimate power must follow this preliminary skirmish between executive and legislature.

When Prince Daud was forced in 1963 to resign the premiership, Dr Yusuf, an able but not very determined man, was appointed and held office as Premier for more than two years until the 1965 elections. When the new Shura met, he was again appointed Prime Minister by the King and with much the same cabinet as before, almost as if there had been no elections. But, surprisingly and encouragingly, the Wolesi Jirgah, raw as it was to the business of parliamentary democracy, showed its teeth, accused some of the members of the Yusuf government of bribery and corruption, and was only with the greatest difficulty persuaded to give its vote of confidence. Certain left-wing members continued to protest and invited the students of Kabul University to come in a body to support their objection. The mass of the students were forcibly restrained from entering the parliamentary building; the inspirers of their demonstration urged them to force their way in* on the following day on the grounds that it was their right to be present. There then broke out the student riots to which we have already referred. This disturbance was largely instrumental in inducing Dr Yusuf to resign —in anguish of conscience, his supporters claimed, at the three deaths which occurred—and Mr Muhammad Maiwandwal was invited to form a government.† But the tension between

* An unquestionable breach of Art. 57, para. 3 of the constitution, which states that 'Nobody may enter the meeting place of the Shura by force'.

† Mr Maiwandwal began his public career as a journalist, and was press adviser to the King and president of the Press Department before it became a ministry. For some years prior to 1965, he served as Afghan ambassador, first in Washington, then in Karachi. Before becoming Prime Minister he was, briefly, Minister of Press and Information in

government and Shura was by no means over, although much less hostile than before.

Mr Maiwandwal submitted his government and its policy for approval, and comfortably got his vote of confidence. He then interpreted the constitution as permitting him to make individual changes in the composition of his cabinet without submitting them for approval to the Wolesi Jirgah. This interpretation he acted on, and he still insists (as I found in conversation with him) that he was correct in so doing. Members of parliament thereupon exercised their right to question ministers and used it to criticise the Prime Minister for making these new appointments without first seeking the approval of the Wolesi Jirgah. However, since debate is not permitted on ministerial replies, they could do nothing more, short of moving a 'specific and direct' vote of no-confidence in the government as a whole (Art. 92)*—and this, in the country's unsettled state, they were reluctant to do.

It can thus be seen that the complete divorce between executive and legislature could lead to eventual deadlock, since the Premier cannot command, as yet, party allegiance in the Shura to implement the legislation he requires; and he has not, fortunately for the country's democratic development, sufficient executive powers to govern without it. We shall study the growth of party politics in the next section of this chapter, but in this context it is worth noting that, since the Premier and his cabinet colleagues are not politicians but ex-administrators almost to a man, they are likely to have some difficulty in adapting themselves to the sometimes frustrating but necessary limitations of a parliamentary democracy. Certainly, the Shura is not yet sufficiently organised to present a coherent and fully effective opposition

Dr Yusuf's government. At the time this book went to press, Mr Maiwandwal was reported to be gravely ill, and his replacement in office was imminently expected.

* Art. 92 specifies that a two-thirds majority is required for winning a vote of no-confidence in the first two legislative terms after promulgation of the constitution; thereafter a majority vote of the members suffices.

to government; and, indeed, the majority of its members would probably not wish so to act at present. But if the government rides rough-shod over parliament in this difficult formative phase, it will be laying up possible trouble for its successors.

The process of legislation in Afghanistan requires the enactment of a bill by both houses of parliament and the royal assent. The government, although no member of it is a member of the Shura, may introduce legislation. Any member of the Wolesi Jirgah may also initiate legislation—although, if his proposals require finance or compensation, he has to make provision for this in his bill. He must also get the support of ten other members. The Meshrano Jirgah, while able to initiate legislation, can ultimately exercise only delaying powers over bills from the Wolesi Jirgah should any dispute between the two houses over an item of legislation be incapable of resolution by a joint committee of their members. The Supreme Court may also introduce legislation within certain limits; in all other respects, the judiciary is completely separate from executive and legislative functions, and is independent of these two powers.* The groundwork for the details of both governmental and private members' legislation is done in committees, as in most Western systems, but the Afghan committees are chosen with perhaps a keener eye than is the case of the British parliament to the members' interests and to their expertise, where this is available.

*

Only after the full legislative process has been completed can the government issue regulations to implement its policies, and these—so the constitution prescribes—must not in any way conflict with the spirit, let alone the letter, of the relevant law (Art. 94, para. 4). While it is not specifically the function of the Supreme Court to interpret the constitution, it is possible for an individual to bring a case against the state and thus challenge government regulations in the light of the law.

* The Supreme Court, as such, does not come into being until October 1967; until then the King is responsible for supervising the judicial system of the country.

In this sense, the Supreme Court will be a court of constitutional appeal, but no provision is made for it to take the initiative in pronouncing acts constitutional or otherwise. Issuing regulations to implement its policies is a government function ordinarily exercised by the individual ministers through the machinery of the respective departments, and is put into operation by the officers of these departments throughout the provinces. The ministers are answerable to the Shura, and both houses have the right to question them. They are also under the direct orders of the Prime Minister.

Mr Maiwandwal interprets his role as Prime Minister in Attleean terms and, as was the case with Attlee, he generally has his own way when this is important to him. While the constitution clearly intends the Prime Minister's role to be primarily one of guidance and overall leadership, it also makes no less clear provision for him to issue specific instructions to ministers if he so wishes (Art. 95, para. 4) and consequently for him to demand their resignations should there be a major clash on policy. Such clashes for the time being are likely to revolve round personalities rather than policies, for in no sense is there an organised opposition to the government, either in the Shura or outside it, which could be collectively regarded as an alternative government. Specific issues may for a time and on an *ad hoc* basis unite in opposition to the government sufficient parliamentarians to check it momentarily in its stride (as over the appointment of Dr Yusuf's cabinet), but of positive and unifying philosophies or even policies there is as yet no sign. Such unifying factors as there are tend to be negative issues like concern over, or involvement in, corruption.

Corruption undoubtedly presents a major and immediate problem in Afghan government. A decision of May 1966 to imprison a judge for taking bribes marks a courageous initial step against the acceptance of corruption as a normal and inevitable ingredient in the Afghan way of life. The problem is to draw a dividing line between corruption and the customarily permissible nepotism—indeed, to know just how far it is practicable to go in the tight-knit society of the Afghan governing classes in breaking down that nepotism in favour of a meritocracy. The Minister of the Interior once pointed out with tolerant cynicism that, within hours of a great set-to at question time in the Wolesi Jirgah, the very deputies who had denounced his supposed corruption* would be round at his office to beg posts for their sons, cousins and nephews.

Such practices are likely to continue as long as the government remains the only considerable source of patronage and as long as parliamentary, ministerial and civil service salaries are so low that they make some form of supplementary income—by private enterprise in some instances, by taking bribes in many others—almost a matter of survival. Moreover, it is unreasonable to expect wholly 'clean' democratic government so long as there is no united opposition ready to replace the government at the first sign of failure. The creation of such an opposition has become a matter of urgency for Afghanistan.

THE AFGHAN POLITICAL SCENE

The Afghan constitution makes clear provision for the growth of political parties (Art. 32, para. 3 *et seq.*), entrusting to the Shura the drafting of a bill to govern their creation. The only constitutional limitations imposed are that such parties must not oppose the values embodied in the constitution (of which the chief are the principles of Islam and of constitutional monarchy) and that their organisation and finances be open to public scrutiny. These parties, however, cannot come into being until the appropriate law is enacted.

It is tempting for the government, faced with so many problems, to delay the passing of a Political Parties Bill and thus ensure for itself a disorganised opposition and the opportunity to pre-empt, perhaps not altogether unjustifiably, the bulk of parliamentary time for its own legislative programme. So far, the government has not resisted this temptation, and at the time of writing (August 1966) the law of the

* I should add that in this instance any such suspicions would be quite unfounded.

country still takes no cognisance of the existence and rights of political parties, although the draft of a Bill is reported to have got to the committee stage. The Maiwandwal administration cannot bear the sole blame for this, for political activity is minimal—though it may be argued that it will remain so until the formation of parties is made legal.

A very strong reason for this situation is to be found in the composition of the Wolesi Jirgah. The standard of debate is poor, the quality of members in general is poorer. There is an enormous contrast between the two or three dozen able members and the rest, the bulk of whom merely fulfil the minimum requirements of sanity, literacy and attainment of their twenty-fifth birthday. For the most part they are small landowners, chosen for their local influence rather than for any wider ability or knowledge. Ultra-conservative in outlook, they yet lack any coherent philosophy of conservatism. It is not simply that the Shura's debates are considerably more disorderly than those of the House of Commons, and its members inexperienced in the art of parliamentary discussion. What is more serious is the lack of any imaginative approach to the country's problems. Although legislators in many a Western state can be just as unimaginative, in Afghanistan this deficiency is not supplied by a strong body of political thinking and an informed public opinion capable of perceiving national needs and the policies necessary to meet them. The initiative lies almost exclusively with the government, apart from a handful of deputies with the ability to devise and present legislative proposals. At present, the members of the administration, while of varying calibre, are generally speaking very able men with plenty of ideas, tempered surprisingly frequently by realism; yet the time will come when they grow stale. The only collective alternative forseeable at the moment would be the Yusuf cabinet, which contained a number of able ministers now relegated to impotent obscurity in the provinces; but, however unjustly to individuals, this alternative group carries a collective label of venality.

★

Is there any immediate prospect, then, of political parties emerging? If they do, what will be the nature of their policy and their support? The present political character of the Wolesi Jirgah, in so far as it can be said to have one at all, is overwhelmingly conservative, but there are two other small groupings, one of which certainly has a strong potential for development into a coherent political party in due course. It is in these groups that most of the more able deputies can be found.

The smallest and least significant is on the extreme left, and consists of Mr 'Babrak' and no more than two or three sympathisers. The path of natural development into a communist party for these neo-Marxists is completely blocked by the constitution, whose stipulation excluding all opposition to Islam clearly rules out an atheist party. In any case, there is no evidence to suggest any strong, or even potential, support in the country for such a party, although it has one or two adherents among the students of Kabul University. These, however, for the time being seem to have been somewhat sobered by the tragic consequences of their last excursion into politics when the student riots of 1965 led to three deaths. Certainly, a nervous government is most anxious to keep them clear of politics and to prevent the student body from obtaining the disproportionate political influence which it has gained in other underdeveloped countries.

These students belong much more naturally to the second group, which centres round the shrewd, able and pleasant personality of Mr Farhang, one of the deputies for Kabul, who gave up a ministerial appointment in order to take part in the genesis of politics in Afghanistan. If you question him about the formation of a political party, he will laughingly tell you that he is a very legalistically minded man and that, since parties are not yet legal, he has taken no steps to form one. Then, watching you with a twinkle, he will add after a pause that, of course, he has sounded his fellow deputies' opinions on political subjects and discovered those who are like-minded. There seems, in fact, to be only about a dozen or fifteen of these 'like-minded' deputies (although, in contesting the office of Secretary of the Wolesi Jirgah, Farhang obtained a quarter of the total votes). The 'like-minded' might be encompassed by the term he uses to indicate his own affiliation with international political elements: 'liberal democratic parties with social tendencies'. Certainly, he and his colleagues draw inspiration from the European social democrats, but more particularly from the progressive parties from such other underdeveloped countries as Burma, India and Egypt. The basis of his economic policy is that the state must play a major role, almost an exclusive one, in the development of the backward economy of such an under-developed nation as Afghanistan, and that the consequence of the need for capital resources to achieve this development must be a policy of neutrality.

The constitution certainly makes provision for this type of policy to be exercised subject to certain limitations (Art. 29) and, paradoxically, it has been at least partially carried out by a government most of whose individual members would look on Farhang himself as a dangerous radical. Farhang also appreciates what the fundamental nature of Afghan politics will be for the next decade. It will be the politics of the intellectuals and not of the masses. Whoever can win the allegiance of the increasing numbers of technocrats who cannot be fitted into the old nepotistic family patterns will gradually establish political ascendancy.

There are also a number of middle-of-the-road deputies who, while not in any way formed into the nucleus of a political party, are at present outside the Farhang orbit. It is quite possible that they will be lured leftwards towards him by the necessity of co-operation to overcome the huge mass of conservative inertia. Alternatively, they may yet produce a leader of their own and so form a third group in the Shura, definably occupying the centre.

Any political approach to the masses, other perhaps than one based on a simple and fanatical dressing up of Islam, can have little hope of success when the national literacy level is only between 5 and 10 per cent and when communications are physically so difficult, and with the radio, and to a considerable extent the press, under government control as state monopolies.

This is not, of course, the long-term picture. Although literacy campaigns (apart from a small one in the army) are non-existent, the thirst for education is growing daily. There is already a tremendous demand from illiterate farmers and peasants for educational opportunities for their children. The political future of Afghanistan in twenty years' time will be in the hands of those like the small boy whom I saw clad in startlingly light-blue clothes, sitting one May evening on the bank of a paddyfield engrossed in doing his homework in a scruffy exercise book. He and the boys like him are now being found places in Afghanistan's rapidly expanding, but still far from adequate, school system. When there is an adult population among whom a substantial minority at least can read and write and add up, then will come the mass circulation press and the mass political movements. Until then, however, party politics is likely to be confined to the few, and elections will continue to be influenced more by the local power of candidates than by the doctrines they stand for. It may well be, therefore, that administrations of a social democratic nature will emerge long before there is any mass social democratic party; and, indeed, a man of Farhang's calibre may well be the first social democrat Premier long before he can command a coherent majority following in the Wolesi Jirgah.

*

Political debate on any large scale outside the Shura is made very difficult by a nervous administration. For example, there appeared in April 1966 a weekly journal called *Khalq* (The People). Its editorial style was slightly hysterical and many of its articles seemed to show the influence of the banned Tudeh Party in neighbouring Persia. This need not, however, have been a permanent defect and, indeed, friends of free expression in the country were privately urging the owner, Muhammad Taraqi, to make his journal more typically Afghan. The government did not give the paper the chance;

after only five issues, it was closed down on the grounds that it violated the constitution, ostensibly in response to demands for its suppression by members of the Shura. No specific charges were made to justify this, but I was told by the head of the government news agency that its advocacy of public owner-ship and the abolition of private property was the specific aspect that was regarded as impugning the constitution. The students and young intellectuals involved in *Khalq* met angrily to discuss its future. Clandestine editions may appear in due course. In the meanwhile, the government has put a number of other small papers out of business by much more subtle methods, such as persuading the editor to resign (under the press laws, no newspaper may be published without an editor).

The government has also intervened to curtail the political activities of the students in Kabul University, and in particu-lar to prevent them from publishing student journals which might shelter left-wing political material. It is thus stamping down on every open and potentially legitimate outlet for the expression of the radical zeal of youth and for the reasoned discussion of political ideas. The effect is to drive such zeal and discussion underground where, in the long run, they can only become sour and dangerous. For the time being, a man like Farhang can both sympathise with and restrain students and intellectuals, but eventually too rigid a suppression of their views is likely to turn them to more extreme sources of inspiration.

The Prime Minister is basically right in saying (as he did in the interview he gave me) that, when political parties emerge in Afghanistan, they will be influenced less by philosophies and policies than by individuals, and that the first parties will take their shape and colour from their leaders. This is borne out by the absence of 'growth-prospects' in the small middle-of-the-road progressive group in the Wolesi Jirgah, which lacks a leader, and by the absence of cohesion in the conservative majority. A certain unity is given to the con-servative group by a shared and rooted objection to all change, but its lack of a common leadership or programme makes it a loosely formed state of mind rather than a potential party.

In the absence of legitimate party organisation, there is a natural tendency for deputies to group together under other influences. By far the most dangerous of these is that of race. In view of the feeling of the provincials that they are the poor country-cousins, and of the minority races' feeling that the Pathans are lording over them to the point of oppression, the existence of a political vacuum is exceedingly dangerous. Once *ad hoc* groupings on ethnic lines had been given an opportunity to stabilise through time and habit, it would be almost inevitable for them to adopt the style of parties when these became legal. The existing racial antagonisms would then have been politically formalised in a way which would make the growth of national unity almost impossible. Parliament would have a permanent Pathan majority and a permanently and increasingly embittered opposition of mutually suspicious minority races. This danger has not yet materialised, but it threatens.

The creation of political parties based on different philosophical concepts and differing programmes for the nation's development could prove the most effective antidote to racialism and ethnic politics. But if the new deputies in the Wolesi Jirgah and the young intellectuals are to find their natural political allegiance in such multiracial groupings or parties, then the government cannot afford to delay over the passing of a Political Parties Bill and in encouraging the expression of different political views, however immature and exasperating—not to say even subversive—these may at first seem. It is, therefore, very necessary for the government to encourage, not repress, every possible medium of political debate if it is genuinely interested, as it almost certainly is, in seeing the democratic system take root.

There are, of course, risks of instability in a sudden, hothouse flourishing of political activity. A rapid upsurge of radicalism could lead to a strong reaction, possibly with military backing, as has occurred elsewhere—not only in the Third World, but in longer-established states. For the time being, at least, the army is content to stay out of politics. It is a highly privileged section of the community in terms of material rewards and prestige. Provided that each ensuing government ensures that it remains so, it is likely to be content with the King's plans for political evolution. The army is not directly involved in politics except in so far as the conduct of the Public Works Department and the administration of the frontier provinces, with their tribal trouble potential, are still in the hands of the military. All the same, it is the only really efficient nation-wide organisation. Although there is no sign that dissident young officers or ambitious colonels wish to overthrow the régime, if the army (and airforce) ever come to the point of seeking to effect a change, there is very little to prevent them from doing so.

These dangers, however, are remote compared with the grave handicap Afghanistan will labour under if, having created a democratic constitution and system of government, it does not allow the essential political activity which goes with them in a free society.

DEMOCRATIC PROSPECTS

There are, of course, criteria other than the existence of political parties for measuring the degrees of democratic freedom prevailing in a country. The position of the press; the conduct of elections; the degree of arbitrariness in the administration of law and government; the inviolability of home and property—all are tests by which we can measure this freedom or the lack of it.

To read the section of the Afghan constitution dealing with the Basic Rights and Duties of the People (Arts. 25–40) is to realise that its drafters were determined to secure these liberties, subject to certain cautious reservations of a modest and reasonable nature. Here one finds guaranteed to the Afghan citizen freedom of unarmed assembly ('unarmed' is a necessary stipulation in Afghanistan); freedom of expression; the right to education, medical care and work; the inviolability of the individual's home and his communications by letter and telephone; his innocence of crime until his guilt is proved and his protection against torture, forced confession or barbarous punishment. He may travel freely within the bounds of his own country and may own property. He is also liable for taxation and military service only as provided by law.

It is hard as yet to make a fair judgement of the extent to which these rights are fully enjoyed, for in many cases the sheer inability of the country to offer the opportunities laid down by the constitution makes such a test impracticable. Education is still largely a male privilege at all levels, and in any case there are still only 239,000 children of primary school age (i.e. up to twelve years) in state schools, which probably represents less than 15 per cent. Moreover, higher education is not quite the path to freedom and enterprise or to intellectual eminence that it might be. (While the standard of the best is very high, the bulk of students in Kabul University are still working, academically, at about fifth-form level in a British grammar school.) The government, through the Ministry of Education, chooses who shall have the scarce places at Kabul University and the very few Technical Institutes; it decides what course of study a student shall follow, and exacts in payment almost a lifetime of compulsory government service from graduates, who may not be free to strike out on their own until their fifties.

Although the health services have done amazing work over the last twenty years in the eradication of malaria (of which 97 per cent of the country is now completely free), tuberculosis, trachoma and other eye diseases, intestinal disorders and water-borne diseases still ravage the majority of the population. One doctor estimates that, of his 200,000 patients, 90 per cent are to some extent suffering from TB. Patients still have to pay for drugs, although doctors often run their own subsidy system, charging wealthier patients heavily and giving drugs free or very cheaply to the poor. Help in the war against disease is being given by UNESCO and other UN agencies, but it will be a long time before the Afghans are free from ignorance, poverty and disease, not because of any lack of will or devotion but for lack of means, which the rich half of the world must largely be responsible for providing.

Yet there are areas in which the genuineness of the democratic intentions of those who hold power in Afghanistan can be assessed. The elections of the autumn of 1965 provide one such touchstone. There were 1,358 candidates for the 215 seats in the Wolesi Jirgah (six of which were reserved for nomads), and 100 for the 28 directly elected seats in the Meshrano Jirgah. By no means all of these candidates were hand-picked nominees of the King and his administration. Many of the elections were quite heatedly contested, and one provincial governor at least (to judge from the interview I had with the governor of Kunduz) had considerable difficulty in keeping alive a warm interest without letting the contest come actually to the boil. On the other hand, the local election commissions did a considerable amount of preliminary screening to ensure that no 'subversive' characters—that is to say, those who might too dramatically oppose the administration's programme—were allowed either to stand as candidates or to vote. The candidates themselves were largely local influential landowners—generally, but not always, of the predominant ethnic group in the locality. Six women candidates put themselves up for election and women were entitled to vote. Four of the women were elected, as we have seen, but the number of women voters was disappointingly small—mainly because husbands and fathers in many cases expressly forbade their womenfolk to participate in this open public activity.

The election campaign gave encouraging evidence of the government's desire for genuine debate between candidates, although in the absence of parties this had to be on a largely personal basis. Newspapers printed the name and picture of every candidate free; candidates were able to purchase both advertising space and air-time on Radio Kabul (at about £12 a minute for a maximum of five minutes); and the radio station itself ran an extensive series of explanatory programmes on how the elections were to work and what they were all about. Throughout the campaign, provincial governors and other prominent local officials spent much time explaining to voters what kind of people they ought to vote for, that is to say, they were soliciting support for candidates sympathetic to the administration. Yet there is no evidence of other direct pressures being brought to bear on the electorate to influence their voting. Clearly, a man had to be able to dip substantially into his own purse to finance a campaign, and this naturally tended to limit candidature to the wealthier sections of the community; but, apart from this practical consideration, the field was open to all comers who could satisfy the qualificatory provisions laid down in the constitution (Art. 46). Considerable pains were taken also with the conduct of the ballot itself, both to ensure its secrecy and its accuracy. Each candidate had a separate ballot box with his name, photograph and electoral symbol on it and into one of these, in the privacy of a screened booth, the voter dropped his ballot paper to indicate his choice.

Despite these efforts, however, the election remained largely confined to intellectuals and city dwellers, as one might expect for the first election among a generally illiterate population. Even in the cities the poll was not high—from 5 to 10 per cent of those eligible to vote—and in the rural areas it was often as little as 2 per cent. Thus we cannot reasonably call the present deputies in the Shura representative of the people as a whole, though they certainly are representative of the politically aware and interested (or organisable), with the towns naturally returning the more radical and unusual members. Moreover, in assessing the poll in rural areas with a very low turn-out of voters, one has to appraise with caution the merits of the multi-ballot-box mode of voting.

Yet the election can be seen as a clear, if limited, success for the democratisers. There was virtually no indication of corruption or coercion; there was a competitive campaign and a fair ballot. The next step must be to extend the interest in elections to as large a part of the adult population as possible. The municipal elections of autumn 1966 have probably gone some way towards doing this, being as they are of more immediate concern to a greater number of people. For the rest, we still have to await the spread of literacy, the appearance of political parties and of a sustained form of debate on the state-controlled radio.

*

Freedom of expression cannot just be measured in terms of an open election campaign. The opportunity for unhampered criticism of the government and sustained argument about the major issues of the day among a wider non-political public is essential. The most common vehicle for such debate is the press, and the degree of freedom it enjoys is an important guide to the general degree of freedom of expression. In Afghanistan, there is little sign yet of a genuinely free press. We have already seen how swift the government is to close down any journal whose views smack of the revolutionary; but for Afghan newspapers and weekly journals there are also other difficulties, the majority of which are circumstantial rather than deliberate government restrictions. The first and most obvious limitation is the level of illiteracy. The total newspaper and magazine circulation of Afghanistan is under 100,000, or something of the order of one paper for every 150 inhabitants. About half of the readership is in Kabul where, moreover, the English language *Kabul Times* accounts for about 8,000 copies. Then again, until recently, the actual physical processes of newspaper production were a government monopoly.

A similar position still exists with the means of gathering and distributing news itself. The government news agency, *Bakhtar*, has just opened up a new national Telex network to speed up its news services, and has a staff of some ninety reporters in Kabul and the provinces. This news service is available to all newspapers on payment of the usual fees, but to accept it is to accept what is virtually government-filtered news. It is not without significance that, on two occasions of critical importance to the government, the head of the news agency was refused permission to leave his post and go abroad. No existing newspaper in Afghanistan can afford to keep up anything like a comparable reporting service of its own. Largely for this reason, Afghan newspapers are rather organs of proprietorial opinion than media for disseminating accurate news. Indeed, no newspaper in Afghanistan is yet a viable economic proposition. This is one of the few fields where the use of foreign capital is extremely difficult since the constitution lays down (Art. 31, para. 4) that only an Afghan may own and publish a newspaper in Afghanistan.* Until Afghanistan has developed a consumer economy, there will be no demand for mass advertising media such as that provided by the press and, therefore, no source of untied finance for the papers themselves. Advertising space is sold in the Afghan press, but largely through a government-created advertising agency. To be fair, the administration, if hostile to press criticism of its actions, seems genuinely to be trying to divest itself of total physical and financial control of the press, and there are now in existence a number of newspapers financed by wealthy individuals. Their circulation and presentation, however, are still more those of a college magazine than of a national or even provincial newspaper.

While the Afghan economic and educational system is in the primary stages of evolution, the alternatives are either private backing by individuals prepared to stand a financial loss to express their personal ideas, or government subsidy— and this latter would involve the support of a number of 'penny-dreadful' news sheets with minute circulation. In this, as in other respects, the appearance of political organisations ready to support a critical, if not unbiassed, press is a matter of urgency. In the meanwhile, the verdict must be that there is not yet a free press in Afghanistan. In physical and economic terms, it is not free because it cannot achieve the necessary financial independence; in editorial terms, it is not free because too sharply expressed criticism of the government can jeopardise its existence altogether.

It would be wilfully pessimistic to despair about the even-

* It should be noted, however, that not only is there a Faculty of Journalism in the University at Kabul but that the help of such outside organisations as the Thomson Foundation has already been sought in the training of Afghan journalists.

tual emergence of a free press in Afghanistan, for freedom of speech is the natural birthright of the Afghan. The pungently expressed views about the government which can be heard in the *chai khanas* are an indication that, when every Afghan can read and write, successive administrations will find themselves appraised with equal vigour on paper.

ADMINISTRATION AND THE LAW

Of far more interest to an illiterate population than the rhetoric of printed debate and the niceties of party politics is the way in which government and law are administered in its immediate neighbourhood.

A good illustration of the practical realities of this system is the story told me by Muhammad Hussein Massa, Governor of Balkh, about 'the tooth that did not fit'. Sitting on his verandah in Mazar-i-Sharif one day, he was suddenly confronted by an agitated citizen who claimed that he had been grievously assaulted and that the Governor must compel his assailant to recompense him financially. The Governor calmed him and bade him sit down and tell his story. This the complainant did with a wealth of graphic detail, his tale reaching its climax with the dramatic production of the tooth which the assailant was supposed to have struck from the victim's mouth.

'Indeed a monstrous blow,' said the Governor, examining the tooth with great solicitude. 'Tell me, from which part of your mouth was it struck? Please show me the wound.'

Taken aback, the complainant thought hastily and then pointed to a gap in his teeth.

'But see,' said the Governor, 'the tooth does not fit. Now stop wasting my time and yours, and go and devote your energy and ingenuity to more useful ends.'

In a still simple society of isolated communities, much depends on the ability, percipience and sympathy of the man on the spot. Afghanistan is fortunately blessed with a wealth of capable administrators throughout the provinces. Indeed, few things impressed me more during my visit in 1966 than

111

the calibre of the many officials I met, at my own request, throughout the country. The Governor of Balkh, it is true, had been the very successful Minister of Mines and Power in the Yusuf administration, in which post he had been largely responsible for the launching of the natural gas industry; but other governors, from Kunduz to Paktya, proved almost without exception to be as able. The governorship of a province is not strictly a civil service type of post; for instance, there is no ban on a governor's continuing to participate in political life while he holds office. The only limitation is the practical one that appointments to provincial governorships are made by the Minister of the Interior.

The provincial governor, almost invariably very short staffed, has a two-pronged administrative machine. The first prong is that of his direct decision-making. The majority of decisions in the practical fields of agriculture, industry, irrigation, mining and so on are reached in conjunction with the representatives on the spot of the appropriate ministries and are not often referred back to Kabul. In this relationship, the governor usually takes the initiative. Both governor and departmental representative are working within the limitation of the budgetry allocation under the particular departmental heading for their province. There is no local revenue, although the national revenue through taxation is gathered as a provincial responsibility. The various ministries are given their share of the national budget and then allocate this to different projects in the provinces. Hitherto, the initiative for these projects has been largely ministerial, although the detail of their application has been worked out at local level, but now the provinces themselves are being encouraged to propose schemes of development. The other prong of the provincial governor's administrative machine is provided through a series of district governors in charge of various sections of his province. They work to his orders and have their own small staff. The more go-ahead provincial governors are now encouraging regular general meetings between all these subordinates to thrash out a co-ordinated policy for all the districts.

An Experiment in Democracy

The system demands that both the greater and the lesser governor be accessible to the people of the province or district. It is a common sight, in the Pathan areas in particular, to find the local district governor being buttonholed in the street (literally, for he is probably the only one wearing European dress) by some loquacious citizen and urged to do or prevent something. Not that the Pathans are spineless beseechers of authority when some grievance exercises their concern; far from it. As one district governor pointed out to me, such is the initiative of the Pathan and his extraordinary capacity for voluntary corporate activity that, as often as not, the job has been done by the time the governor has even heard that it needs to be done.

The dialogue between governor and governed is to be formalised through elected Provincial Councils, starting with the municipal elections in the autumn of 1966. But even when these Councils are formed and have chosen their chairman, in most provinces the real power and initiative will still lie mainly in the hands of the governor. The remarkable thing is that the governors are quite willing to be guided in many things by public opinion in the various forms in which it is expressed to them.

The provincial governor's other important responsibility is for the local police. He can also call in the military if he thinks its help to be necessary in maintaining public order, but he has no direct authority over the military in his province. The picture in this respect is a little ambiguous in those Pathan tribal areas where the administration is military and the governor a senior military officer, although at district level the military administrator acts to all intents and purposes as a civilian. A further confusion is likely to arise with the creation of a police investigation department directly responsible to the Attorney-General's office and not to the provincial governor's. A certain amount of antagonism is already evident as a result of this division. The local police feel that, despite their particular knowledge of the area, they are being relegated to an inferior peace-keeping position. The Attorney-General's department, by contrast, views its activities as an independent

113

assurance of the objective investigation of a charge or a crime. The representative of the Attorney-General acts rather in the capacity of the French 'juge d'instruction', as both prosecutor and judge in examinations of first instance, but it is always open to the accused to appeal from his decisions to a higher court. Similarly, a tribesman could technically appeal to his district governor against a fine inforced by the local Jirgah, but he would get short shrift from governor and fellow citizens alike in most cases. A determined man could take the matter still further by appeal to the provincial governor or to the courts.

★

The police forces, generally unarmed, and their members— mostly Pathans—vary considerably throughout the country. There are plenty whose sole concern is to ensure that, if you are going to get your throat cut or meet with any other mishap, this must happen on someone else's territory; so you must be moved on as rapidly as possible to the next district. On the other hand, there are also many policemen, often of very junior rank, who will go to enormous pains to ensure, not only your safe sojourn and passage in their village or town, but your comfort and convenience also. The Afghans are probably the world's most hospitable people and do not shed their customs when they don the rather scruffy, faded blue uniforms of the police force.

The major legal problem in Afghanistan has been to ensure the application of a 'common' law to all parts of the country: a problem arising, not so much from abuse—although in the past the Afghan judiciary has certainly been open to corruption—as from tribal customs. In Pathan districts, the law has been a combination of custom and personal justice assessed by the local Jirgah, or Council. It worked very often on the basis of 'everybody knows that so-and-so did such-and-such' rather than on careful accumulations of evidence. It contained a highly compensatory rather than a purely punitive element, and was much concerned with personal honour. The story of the old woman who, when her great-nephew could not produce the blood-money to absolve him from the murder of a member of another family, threw on to the ground the exact sum, untouched, which that family had paid her grand-father as blood-money, illustrates the persistence of the 'customary law'.

In all these frontier districts, the Afghan government has been trying gradually to replace a patchwork of different customs with a common law which does not sacrifice the element of true justice in the Jirgah system or so antagonise the local tribesmen that they ignore the courts and revert to personal revenge. It seems that the authorities are having considerable success in this. One district governor told me that in his area, which included the villages of the fierce and hitherto unruly Mangals, there had been in the previous five years no murders and only one case of manslaughter (the accused was a child). This view was confirmed by the fact that our party, including two women, was permitted in 1966 to travel in these tribal areas without any escort, which would not have been the case a decade ago.

A number of factors contribute to this acceptance of central and common control. In the first place, it is administered by those who, like the tribesmen themselves, are fighting men—that is to say, by the Afghan army. Then again, central authority has clearly brought with it a number of material improvements—in agricultural techniques, communications, medicine and education—so that the new ways as a whole are being gradually identified as beneficial. Finally, the tribal Jirgah has not been suddenly deprived of power and influence but rather has had its function changed to that of a local government council concerning itself with local construction and irrigation projects, and with disputes over property, the use of irrigation water and so on.

This is not to say that nationally administered law is completely accepted by all except a criminal class. The administrative arm of the law still does not stretch into every corner of the country. But events like those following the case in Badakshan in 1964, when three Germans were shot by local villagers (one of the Germans, left for dead, photographed the assassins, made his way back to Kabul and developed the picture which led to the capture and execution of the murderers), are slowly creating a general recognition of the rule of a central and common law.

The national code of criminal procedure is now under revision. That drawn up under the 1964 constitution is based on French practice, modified in the light of Egyptian experience; indeed, Egyptian legal advisers have assisted in its drafting. The current revision is intended to bring the code still more into line with specifically Afghan needs.

The acceptance of fairly wholesale changes in laws and customs does not in the long run depend on any abstract intellectual acceptance of their appositeness. Acceptance depends on their being seen as part of a general evolution which is beneficial to the ordinary people of Afghanistan. The most obvious measure of the beneficence or otherwise of that evolution is in its ability to improve the material standards of the Afghans. It is not too much to say that on the success of economic development in the next twenty years all else depends.

7

The Arithmetic of Progress

FOUR OUT OF EVERY FIVE Afghans earn their living from
the land in some way, and Afghanistan depends for its exports,
which in 1965 reached only half the level of its imports, on
agricultural produce and the cottage industries associated
with it. For the foreseeable future, economic progress must
largely depend on the expansion and improvement of agriculture. Yet four-fifths of the land area of Afghanistan—a
country three times the size of England and Wales—is desert.

These deserts are not all immutable, and many of them in
the west and south-west of the country were once highly fertile
irrigated areas. Although not as easily as was once hoped, they
can be rendered fertile again by the waters of those deserts of
snow and ice high in the Afghan mountain ranges. In much of
Afghanistan there is good soil but no water, while where there
is water the soil is poor or non-existent. The basic problem
for Afghanistan is to mate soil and water to fertility.

It is a problem which has been clearly recognised by
successive Afghan governments in the past decade, and
already steady progress in the development of irrigation and
hydroelectric power has been made. A number of major
projects, Nangarhar (11,000 kw and 25,000 hectares irrigated),
Naghloo (66,000 kw—no irrigation yet) and Mahipar (44,000
kw—no irrigation yet), have just been completed. As the
Second Five Year Plan draws to a close, there are already
3,100,000 hectares under irrigation and a generating capacity
of 192,000 kw in Afghanistan. This is only a beginning, however, for only 12 per cent of potential agricultural land is being
utilised, and of this only a little over a third is irrigated.* The

* The report of the Nathan Institute in 1965 estimated that 5·3
million hectares could be irrigated.

I   117 problem of bringing water to the land is a major preoccupation at every level, from those perhaps over-ambitious dreamers who in the north have initiated surveys to dam the Oxus and use its waters for irrigation, to the peasant who is trying to divert the water of a passing mountain stream to a few square yards of land.

An elderly Pathan, steel-rimmed spectacles perched authoritatively on the end of his nose, accosted me one morning as we made breakfast camp in Paktya. His problem and his solution were typical—as was his belief that, since I was a European, I must be an engineer. He wanted to raise water some six or eight feet from the small river which flowed twenty yards from his land to irrigate a bare patch about the size of a tennis court. He had brought with him a couple of dozen neighbours (typically willing to join in a voluntary co-operative effort of this kind), and he hoped, by piling boulders across the river opposite the top end of his field, to divert sufficient water to it. However, even he had slight doubts about the feasibility of this. The river was swift but shallow, and at that point the water would have had to be raised considerably; yet in debouching from a gorge higher up it made a shallower dam further upstream impossible. It was at this juncture that he consulted one highly unqualified British 'engineer'. No hydrodynamicist, it nevertheless occurred to me that, if only something as simple as a heavy concrete beam with the open ends of half a dozen plastic pipes embedded in it had been available, it might have been lodged in the fast-moving river well above the point at which it was wanted and the water led by flexible pipe to the field as required. Such gadgets were not available and one could only talk about the best spot for the primitive boulder dam. We left our bespectacled friend noisily issuing orders to his neighbours to begin the work. I never knew if it achieved its object, but on its success or failure and on the success or failure of a thousand little enterprises like it much depends for Afghanistan today.

*

The Arithmetic of Progress

AGRICULTURE AND INDUSTRY

The province of Paktya as a whole presents an Afghan agricultural success story. Under its military government, it has not only achieved agricultural success but a considerable social triumph as well in persuading the belligerent tribesmen to leave their guns at home and cultivate the fields. Certainly they are better fed and more comfortable in leading such a life because the Afghan agricultural authorities are showing the way to steadily improving yields. This is particularly true in the Khost region of Paktya, whence came many of the rebellious tribesmen who unseated Amanullah in 1929.

The government agricultural project in Khost covers an area of 1,200 *jeribs**—about 2,320 square kilometres. Laid out in orderly fashion, it sets a fine example to the equally flourishing private agriculture which surrounds it. Driving through the area, one is immediately impressed by the richness of the crops standing in the fields compared with the bedraggled wisps which struggle in many an acre elsewhere in Afghanistan. Young fruit trees, in which the project specialises, are sent all over the country to start new plantations. The project boasts a small veterinary and artificial insemination station, and two handsome Swiss bulls from which it is hoped to start local dairy herds. An ever-increasing quantity of raw silk is produced, and the soft fruit is of a delicacy and flavour which has to be tasted to be believed. Pesticides and chemical fertilisers, though rarely needed, are freely available to the local farmers and no compulsion is necessary in getting them used; in this part of the world a little neighbourly 'pressure' on any backslider is quite sufficient.

Everywhere in Khost there is a picture of increasing plenty, but just how great an increase? Speculating, probably quite accurately, on the basis of his own experience, the head of the government project—and this is very much an all-Afghan enterprise—claims a 60 per cent average increase in yield per

---

* A *jerib* is an area measurement whose value seems to vary widely throughout the country. Here it equals 44 metres square, I was told by the head of the project.

acre for all the many crops grown in the area since the project was launched in Khost fifteen years ago. But if you ask him the total area under cultivation in Khost, he readily admits that he does not know. This is one of the fundamental drawbacks both to the foreigner's attempt to assess the extent of Afghan achievements and to the Afghans' planning for their future. There are practically no reliable statistics on which to base calculations. There has been no census of population and no agricultural census, although these are now to be undertaken as a matter of priority. While accurate information on financial matters—such as public expenditure, foreign trade and banking, and on industrial production and education—is now generally available, all other figures have at best to be based on sample surveys. Afghan statistics as a whole have to be treated, therefore, with reservation.

In Paktya, however, one can draw a fairly accurate picture of the more prosperous Afghan farmer and the government agricultural worker. The small farmer works on average an area of five *jeribs* (9,680 square metres). This will yield him an income of some 10,000 afghanis a year—which compares very favourably with the Afghan industrial worker (see page 122 below)—and in addition allows him to be his own boss: an important factor in a land of such fiercely independent people. The Afghan farmer is taxed on his land at so much per *jerib* (in Khost, the rate is a modest 6 afghanis), and the larger local landowners act as tax collectors. I was amused to note that, although the police are empowered to assist in tax collection, my question as to what happened if anyone defaulted was met with the unlikely reply: 'Oh, no one ever fails to pay their tax on demand.' The government agricultural worker earns 7,000 afghanis a year, which puts him below his male industrial colleagues. Most of these workers would like to buy land of their own, but new land is not coming under cultivation sufficiently fast to bring the price down; however frugal, the agricultural worker has no hope of saving the 100,000 afghanis he would need to buy his five *jeribs*. Nor is this a situation that can be remedied by expropriating 'land reform', for the greater part of the land is already owned by small proprietors whose holdings could not advantageously be broken up.

It is just possible that he might begin to make his money from freelancing in the timber trade. The hills in Paktya are an impressive sight, stretching for miles and miles with trees dotted over their entire surface, but rather sparsely, standing each three or four yards from its neighbour, the whole looking like a hesitantly gathering crowd. The timber in the past has been haphazardly felled and cultivated scarcely at all, but now a group of West German forestry experts are launching a major forestry project near Ali Khel which should make timber a valuable Afghan export, especially to Pakistan. There is already a steady, if unofficial, trade in camel-borne cedar baulks which fetch in Peshawar or Kohat three or four times what they can be sold for to the Kabul merchants. The government has talked of stopping the trade but, like preventing the extensive two-way smuggling with Pakistan, this would probably be both well-nigh impossible and unwisely provocative.

Paktya is not, of course, the only prosperous agricultural area in Afghanistan. As was noted in chapter 3, there are developments in the Helmand Valley; and the main areas for the cultivation of cotton—Afghanistan's chief cash crop—in Kataghan, round Mazar-i-Sharif and in the province of Kunduz are also agriculturally prosperous, as are the Herat and Jalalabad regions. Indeed, Khanabad in Kunduz claims to be 'the seed gourd of Afghanistan'.

The development of cotton production has been a disappointment to the Afghans for, despite a very rapid increase in yield to 60,000 tons in 1965, the output for the Second Five Year Plan has fallen 62 per cent below the target of 159,000 tons per annum, and this leads one to doubt whether the still greater output of some 200,000 tons* envisaged for the Third Five Year Plan can be attained.

*

* The Third Plan was not yet published at the time of writing but this figure was given to me by the Minister of Agriculture.

Nevertheless, it is on cotton processing that Afghanistan's industrial expansion has principally relied in recent years, with the establishment of gins, presses and oil extraction plants and now of an oil-processing plant. Chief agent of this expansion has been the Spinzar Company ('Spinzar' means white gold): a combination of private and state enterprise in which the controlling power lies with the state. It is astonishing to see the transformation which a single enterprise such as this can bring to the remote towns and villages strung out along the Oxus. It is no exaggeration to claim that in this area virtually every hospital and most schools and housing projects are due to the stimulus or actual creation of the Spinzar Company. This should be remembered when considering the not overgenerous terms on which Spinzar employs its labour.

The basic working week of the Afghan industrial worker is one of 48 hours and the conditions of work—at least in the factories I visited—were very reasonable in normal weather but not, I imagine, comfortable in extremes of heat and cold. For his labour, the well-established but unskilled Afghan worker receives from 900 to 1,000 afghanis a month, although he may start out on as little as 15 to 20 afghanis a day. In the Spinzar Company, however, he will also have access to free medical treatment and in some cases subsidised industrial compound housing of above average quality as well. On the other hand, on one occasion in Khwaja-i-Gar I was told that, since a generator had broken down the factory gates had been locked, and the workers would not be paid for the days of enforced idleness. When I challenged the senior representatives of the company in Kunduz on this, they said that normal practice was to pay for lay-offs of this kind. The Afghan worker lacks effective or militant trade unions to take up his cause, although they would be perfectly legal under the constitution. Wages in fact are negotiated on an individual contract basis with no limits on hire or fire. A good man can, of course, negotiate himself into a relatively strong position, and a really top-line foreman, for example, might earn between 2,000 and 3,000 afghanis a month. This is more than is earned by most doctors or senior civil servants, either of whom might have to pay as much as 1,000 afghanis a month for a government-allocated and not necessarily superior house. The weaker, less able worker, by contrast, may soon find himself dismissed—not that the arbitrariness is by any means all on the employer's side, for the Afghan industrial worker is prone to impulsive fits of absenteeism.

There are scarcely a dozen factories in the Western sense in the whole of Afghanistan in 1966. A sugar factory at Baghlan, a textile mill and a cement factory at Pul-i-Khumri, a porcelain pottery in Kunduz, the cotton-processing factories near Kandahar, a few small plants in Kabul—these provide the sole industrial opportunities in Afghanistan. (There were probably less than 10,000 industrial workers in Afghanistan in 1966.) The equipment in these factories, although in many cases now being replaced by new models from Russia and the West, has been, and sometimes still is, of very ancient vintage. The soap-making in the Spinzar plant at Kunduz, for instance, is done with German equipment dating back to 1928. Thus, the Afghan industrial worker has no mass-production traditions behind him and is, in fact, just a retrained agricultural worker. He does not take easily to the disciplined regularity of modern industrial work, to the clocking in and out, and the necessity of keeping pace with a continuous production process. When harvest time comes round, as often as not he will down tools and dash back to the fields where he can earn for a few weeks as much as 40 afghanis a day and all found. Harvest over, he is outside the factory gate again asking for his job back.

What kind of worker does the Afghan make, then, when he is *on* the job? The answer probably lies somewhere between the assertion of the rather embittered West German engineer who claimed that the Afghans were quite unteachable and that even the technicians forgot everything they had ever learnt when they got back from abroad, and the claim of the Afghan supervisor that his men were 'absolutely marvellous'. The more objective judgement of the Russian engineer in charge of cotton machinery installation was that they took much training but once trained were good workers. It seems to take about a year to train the quite ordinary semi-skilled worker in one of the cotton processing jobs, not because of any lack of native ability but through training difficulties. The only training centre outside Kabul is a German-sponsored technical college at Kandahar, though a Russian-backed college for petroleum technology is planned in Mazar. The great bulk of the training, therefore, is of the on-the-job kind; and on-the-job training of illiterate peasants, using a variety of machines whose instructions are in any case printed in a number of different foreign languages, is not easy and is of necessity oral and slow. And yet, although in formal terms the Afghans have yet to show any outstanding aptitude for technology, they have a positive genius for mechanical improvisation. Vehicles are kept running which in Europe or America would long have rusted away on the scrap heap. They seem able to make do and mend almost indefinitely: a valuable asset in a country where shortage of foreign exchange often makes spare parts virtually unobtainable. It should not, therefore, prove too difficult to adapt this instinctive appreciation of mechanical functions to the more routine applications of industrial society.

The real problem is not one of techniques and training, of native ability or lack of it, but of attitude: the attitude—by no means confined to Afghanistan, a modern Briton must admit—of 'why work if there is a chance of getting rich quickly by speculation or gambling'. To the speculative criteria in Afghanistan is added a positively Micawberish expectation that something will turn up. This problem was graphically described to me by the Governor of Balkh, who is already making plans for the industrial expansion which he believes is certain to take place in his province in the next few years given the recent discovery there of natural gas resources. He sees the labour problem as essentially one of creating a new kind of social responsibility appropriate to a modern society, responsibility to the family, the village, the country. Opportunity for initiative and incentives for seizing it must be swiftly introduced to the ordinary man to 'remove a fatalistic satisfaction with the *status quo*'. Wishful thinking, centred on speculation and gambling, has to be removed and replaced by a desire to work. There will be plenty of employment opportunities in the region in the next few years, and the Governor has asked the local chiefs to persuade their young men to work on the new gas pipeline—adding with a laugh, but with a glint of determination, that if they won't go willingly he is quite ready 'to drive them out of the *chai khanas*', where they sit and gossip the day away. Quite how he will achieve this in a country where forced labour is illegal, I don't know, but I am sure he will and in so doing tackle a fundamental problem in Afghanistan's economic development. Somehow, by incentive or coercion, the Afghan in general has to be persuaded to give up his life of poverty-stricken ease for the sweat of greater affluence.

A further important feature about Afghanistan's industrial workers is that the great majority of them are Pathans, even in the non-Pathan areas. Here they are often members of those families who were moved into non-Pathan provinces as agricultural settlers and were never quite able to fit happily into the local community. Thus, if an industrial élite is to emerge in due course, it looks, on present evidence at least, as if it will be as Pathan-dominated as the administrative élite.

*

But large-scale industrial activity is for the future; for the present the vital considerations are the quantities of wheat, cotton and rice, Karakul skins, wool woven into carpets, and dried fruit which the country can produce to feed itself and for export. These things are not easy to nurture in the harsh climate of Afghanistan. If the winter is too severe and late, it affects the Karakul lambs; if it is too mild and ends too early with little rain, then it fails to keep down the grubs which destroy the grass roots. If the herds and flocks are too small, there is not enough wool for the carpets; if they are too large and graze indiscriminately, then the earth is stripped bare and erosion sets in. If there are too few donkeys, then there is too little transport for what is grown; if there are too many donkeys, they destroy the vegetation. The need is for better husbandry, improved strains of seed and livestock and the development of the appropriate small-scale machinery, such as motorised hand tractors. In the past there have been too many generously given and totally useless normal farm tractors rusting in old forts, and even by the roadside, because they were far too large to use on the Afghan's typically small plot. All these agricultural improvements require capital and the Afghan small farmer does not have it; but the government, with the help of the World Bank, is now making far greater credit facilities available to him. Despite all the obstacles and the need to maintain an ecological balance, Afghan agriculture is steadily improving and its chief products are reaching the markets of the world in ever larger quantities.

Afghan carpets are famous. There is far more to their complex individual production than the weaving referred to in chapter 5, although estimates as to the labour involved in this process vary from those given by the carpet makers on the spot in Chahardarra to the official figure of four women weaving 10 square metres of carpet in a month. Before the wools can be woven, they go through an elaborate process of vegetable dyeing; a host of wild herbs and flowers are available to produce the acid and alkaline dyes in all the many shades that go into the Afghan carpet. Just over half a million square metres of carpet are produced annually, and of this four-fifths are exported—principally to England and West Germany, often via Russia. The value of the carpets exported in 1964 was 462 million afghanis.

Equally beautiful and lucrative are the thousands of Karakul skins, or Persian lambs, which find their way to Afghan heads and rich female shoulders all over the world. (The chief overseas market today is New York, which since the war has displaced London as the main outlet.) The skins—black, brown, grey, gold and, rarest of all, white—are of fine quality. The gold skins, with their infinite changes of shade and light, must surely be the inspiration for the Jason legend. Some 10 million Karakul skins are sold abroad annually and fetch around $17 million in export earnings. Golden fleeces indeed! The Karakul farmer does not perhaps gain his fair share of these rich rewards. The government has established a co-operative marketing system through which the skins are bought at a fixed price, according to grade, that is very substantially below the real market price. The purpose of this, says the government, is to assure the farmer of a regular stable price outlet for his skins under all circumstances, but clearly it is also designed to make money for the government. If the quality and quantity of Karakul skin production is to be maintained, the price to the farmer himself will have to be substantially increased in the next few years.

Other major agricultural exports are cotton (36,000 tons a year, mainly to the Soviet Union) and the fruit one sees drying in the sun on the flat mud roofs of the Afghan villages. But these pay for scarcely half of Afghanistan's essential imports; the remainder have to be bought through money provided by foreign aid and by borrowing from Da Afghanistan Bank (see Appendix II for Export and Import Tables). The remaining cottage industries—leather working, sheepskin jackets, and the delightfully intricate pieces of hand-beaten copper—are important only for saving scarce foreign currency by supplying the domestic market.

Tourism could be a source, hitherto unexploited, of foreign exchange. Afghanistan—likened to Switzerland by Sir Olaf Caroe—not only contains some of the most beautiful and impressive scenery in the world but also a wealth of sites of historical and cultural interest. As communications by road and air improve, many of these will become more accessible. If the hostelries in country towns could be got to provide, in *working* order, those amenities which tourists expect, without spoiling the local flavour of food and services, Afghanistan would become a very attractive holiday spot for the moderately rich traveller.

For any major industrial expansion, however, Afghanistan must look to resources other than cottage industry and tourism.

Afghanistan

DEVELOPMENT POTENTIAL AND
FORWARD PLANNING

Striking it rich is the dream of every underdeveloped country hoping to solve all the problems of capital for development. If not on a bonanza scale, two major discoveries in Afghanistan in the past few years bear rich promise for the future: natural gas at Shiberghan in the Balkh province, and iron ore at Hajigak in Bamian.

The volume of gas at Shiberghan is estimated at 500 million cubic metres a year and it is planned, eventually, to pipe the gas off in two directions. One pipeline is to go north to the Soviet Union. The export of gas to Russia will have the valuable effect of making the Afghan economy a little less dependent on charity from that source, since Afghanistan will be able eventually to pay for far more of what it needs from its neighbour. The other will go south towards Hajigak, and along its route factories are to be established using the pipeline as a source of power. The first factory planned is a fertiliser plant in Mazar-i-Sharif itself, 110 kilometres from the gas source, which is expected to produce 56,000 tons of fertiliser a year and should be in production by 1967. The terminus of this second pipeline may eventually be in the Hajigak area for the phased development of a steel industry.

It has been estimated by an Afghan survey that the iron-ore deposit at Hajigak amounts to 2,000 million tons of a very high grade (62 per cent iron content is the official estimate). Moreover, only a few miles away there is a substantial deposit of limestone for use in iron-ore smelting. Even so, despite the tempting juxtaposition of all the necessary ingredients, the Afghan government is being hard-headed and realistic in appraising the advisability or otherwise of launching its own steel industry, and extensive feasibility studies are being made before any final decision is reached. The responsible ministers are aware that the present scale of Afghan industrial development, the limited prospects of export of steel to neighbouring countries, and the inadequate development of the transport system for a large-scale export of iron ore, would not justify tying up any large sum of scarce capital in the crash development of the industry. They are far more likely to go in for stage-by-stage exploitation as their own domestic demands justify it.

Extensive traces of other mineral deposits have been found throughout Afghanistan but none of these is really substantial, apart from a large sulphur deposit near Nangarhar. Coal is mined in small quantities in a dozen places, but the largest deposit—at Shalashak in Balkh province—does not exceed 25 million tons. Lead, manganese, marble, gypsum, barite, gold and beryl have all been found. As one might expect in this part of the world, oil has also been discovered but so far there has been nothing more encouraging than the 8 to 9 million tons estimated at Saripul—far less than the reserves of the rich fields of Persia and southern Russia. One of the oldest mining operations in Afghanistan is for the semi-precious and very beautiful lapis lazuli found only in the remote mountain regions of Badakshan, where some of the mines are so high that they can only be worked in summer. Between 30 to 40 tons of this ultramarine stone, shot through with threads of gold, are mined each year.

The development of all these mineral resources with just the right balance of proportion between them will require a very sophisticated level of planning in a country where both private and state capital are in short supply. The co-ordination needed will demand a high degree of central control, and it is this control which the Ministry of Planning is designed to exercise.

*

Afghanistan is, I think, untypical of many underdeveloped countries in the degree of realism that its government brings to the problems of planning: realism, that is, within the political context which enables it to count on very substantial sums of aid, principally from Russia, but also from the United States.* Not that Afghan planning is without its

* The clear declaration of American policy (at the opening of the final section of the Kandahar–Kabul highway in July 1966) for the administration of PL 480 must, therefore, have come as something of a

fiascos; the great international airport at Kandahar, at which none of the international jets actually touches down, is a prize white elephant in anyone's catalogue. But, generally speaking, an unostentatious sense of real priorities has prevailed. This is largely due to the able men who have worked in the planning and financial departments, and in particular to the Finance Minister, Mr Yaftali—the only significant survivor from the Yusuf cabinet—and the Deputy Minister of Planning, Mr Haidar. Their philosophy is summed up in the preamble to the Second Five Year Plan: 'Unlike some other developing countries, where economic policy is conditioned by a preconceived ideology, planning in Afghanistan emanates from certain basic facts of the economy.'

The first two Five Year Plans, the second of which runs to March 1967, were naturally enough concerned with the development of infrastructure projects, such as those for roads, irrigation and hydroelectric power which have been referred to earlier. Progress on these has been largely as predicted, although official documents, particularly those issued to visitors, do sometimes tend to confuse intention with accomplishment. There have been one or two major short falls, such as that in cotton production, but by and large the picture is one of only a moderate falling short of targets right across the board. This pattern has been the result of deliberate policy. The two major obstacles to fulfilment of the Plan have been the shortage of capital, as we have already seen, and the shortage of skilled personnel. Indeed, this latter factor has led to the ironic situation in which capital-hungry Afghanistan has had to turn down some offers of foreign credits because of the lack of the necessary skilled manpower to take advantage of them. The planners' reaction to this situation has been to cut back a little on many projects rather than bring any one section to a complete standstill.

shock to the Afghans. Those countries that are estimated to have the capacity to increase their own food production will now be expected to pay for food aid under this law. At the time of writing, the declaration was too recent for one to judge how hard-heartedly it would, in fact, be put into practice.

The Arithmetic of Progress

The most striking feature of the Second Five Year Plan is the extent to which certain sectors are almost entirely financed from foreign aid. In education, in the Helmand Valley project and in the press department development scheme, foreign assistance accounts for over 90 per cent of investment, and it is just under 90 per cent for health and civil aviation. (For full details of investment and finance sources of the Second Five Year Plan, see Appendix III). The Plan sensibly states that on the success of agricultural development all else depends, yet the investment proportions for agriculture and industry in the Second Plan are 23·5 per cent and 33·5 per cent respectively. Not too much should be made of this disparity, however, since on projects such as hydroelectric-irrigation schemes any categorisation is inevitably arbitrary.

Another feature of the Plan likely to strike a Western observer is the minute proportion of the investment burden under the Plan to be carried by the private sector, amounting as it does to only 0·6 of one per cent. This is at least partially explained by the fact that the Plan is mainly concerned with large government-controlled infrastructure projects, in which there is no opportunity for the private investor. But it is nevertheless surprising that private investment in the Second Plan was attracted only to the Departments of Mines, Agriculture, Commerce and the Municipalities. Such likely fields for private capital as civil aviation, communications and the press made no provision for its participation.

One other important factor is the dog that does not bark in the night. There is no mention of military expenditure or the amount of Russian aid devoted to it; but, of an annual domestic revenue of 4,200 million afghanis, only some 3,000 million are expended under the Plan, which in itself covers most major areas of expenditure. (This figure of 3,000 million is an average annual figure based on the 15,000 million afghanis budgeted as coming from domestic sources for the duration of the Second Five Year Plan.) There is thus left 1,200,000 afghanis a year for the remaining items of expenditure and for military expenditure.

Considering that the Afghan-met proportion of the military

131

budget probably only covers payment for personnel, buildings, maintenance, transport, etc., and that the bulk cost of arms and equipment is met by Russia, the proportion of Afghanistan's revenues—one guesses about 30 per cent—consumed by military spending is staggering. Understandably, since the days of Nadir Shah, the régime has never again permitted itself to be caught without adequate military strength to enforce its authority if needs be. It has also to be recognised that in the Pathan border areas the military also carries out the functions of a civil administration. However, it is abundantly clear that the creating of a strong sense of national unity and of good relations with neighbouring Pakistan, so that military expenditure can be substantially reduced, are cardinal factors in Afghanistan's economic as well as in its social development.

The Third Five Year Plan is not due to come into operation until March 1967. At the time of writing (August 1966), the draft of it—virtually completed from the point of view of the staff of the Ministeries of Planning and Finance—has yet to be discussed at ministerial and parliamentary level. In frank discussions with the officials and ministers chiefly concerned, I gained the impression that a number of sensible changes of emphasis are envisaged. Now that the major infrastructure projects are completed or nearing completion, and once the carry-over obligations from the Second Plan are met, there will be a very considerable switch to smaller scale projects that give a swift return on investment. It is hoped to attract private domestic capital as the main source of finance for these. A figure as high as 30 per cent of the total investment for the Third Five Year Plan was mentioned by Mr Haidar as the possible proportion to be carried by the private sector. It is hoped, too, to attract additional private foreign capital by the concession of tax holidays and the absence of controls on remittances home. The clause of the constitution preventing foreigners from owning immovable property in Afghanistan might act as a deterrent to such investment. (Art. 29, para. 6.)

Then again, the investment in the agricultural sector is to

be increased, although it is pointed out that in a sense the industrial investment in basic facilities which took place in agricultural areas under the Second Five Year Plan could also be said to be agricultural investment. However, such investment is now to be even more direct, with a greater proportion of the budget put straight into agriculture. In the development of industry, priority is to be given to those industries that process local agricultural produce. The rate at which new land can be brought under cultivation is limited by the large capital cost of irrigation projects, so equal emphasis is to be given in the Third Five Year Plan to the intensification of agricultural production through mechanisation and improved techniques. One consequence of this must be to reduce the need for agricultural labour, and this will either increase hidden unemployment or stimulate the movement of labour into industry.

*

None of these planning decisions and assessments can be considered in a pure economic vacuum. The really crucial questions are whether the planning of the economy has made and will make the ordinary Afghan better off. It is difficult to answer these questions in the absence of reliable statistics. A doctor will speak of extensive malnutrition, while the evidence of one's eyes suggest that food is both good and relatively cheap and plentiful. Kebabs and kormas with plenty of meat, flat discs of coarse tasty bread and bowls of rice, salt and spices, fruit from apricots to melons, high quality tomatoes and cucumbers—all seem plentiful. On the other hand, the visual evidence of disease is also plentiful. Rarely does one see an Afghan in rags, or the rows of sleeping beggars which are a common sight in such Asiatic cities as Calcutta, but the drainage and water supply are almost invariably unhygienic and inadequate.

During the last two years of the First Plan and the early part of the Second Five Year Plan, there was a very steep rise in the cost of living as the result of heavy deficit financing. The cost of living index, based at a 100 in 1960, had risen by

1964 to 151: a rate of increase of 10 per cent per annum.* As a result, however, of stern measures to reduce the budgetary deficit, this rise in living costs has been reduced dramatically to between 3 and 4 per cent in each of the past two years, at which rate the Finance Minister now hopes to be able to peg the inflationary trend. The government has also set up a special commission on prices, one of whose functions is to try to steady the price of food by purchase during glut and by releasing stocks on to the market when there is any sign of scarcity.

Gradually, too, the tax structure is being used as an instrument of social justice as well as a means of raising revenue. There have recently been quite sharp increases in the rate of land tax (doubled) and of direct income tax, which between them account for about 20 per cent of domestic revenue. The bulk of government revenue, however, is still derived from customs duties, from tax on foreign exchange transactions (which amount to about a third of the total revenue), and from government monopolies and enterprises. It is impossible to measure the rate of growth of the Afghan GNP, although this deficiency will be remedied during the Third Five Year Plan, but the guess hazarded by the Finance Minister is 54,000 million afghanis in 1966.

Afghanistan is a country which is certainly poor, but poor without that desperation which characterises so many other underdeveloped countries. Its economy is expanding, fitfully but substantially, as more and more of the conventional economic tools become available to government and to administrators who seem quick to learn to use them skilfully. But major economic advance still depends on large injections of foreign capital, which will almost certainly be forthcoming, and on an adequate supply of skilled manpower, for which sufficient provision has still probably not been made. If there is ever a revolution in Afghanistan, the odds are just marginally in favour of its not being one inspired by hungry bellies.

* This rise may have been exaggerated somewhat by the fact that the price changes recorded were mainly urban.

8

Prospects for the Future

THE CHANGES in Afghanistan over the last ten years have
been far-reaching. Now you can travel round the country,
between the main centres, both swiftly and safely. You can
see a woman's face as she passes you in the street, and drink
Scotch with a provincial governor and his guests on the
verandah of his house. You can turn on a light and pick up a
telephone in many a remote village. The Russian engineer you
may meet there will now talk freely with you. You can hear a
heated debate in a democratically elected parliament and almost forget that an autocratic monarchy, governing through a
family oligarchy, ever existed.

These are dramatic changes, but are they any more significant than the things which have not changed?: the generosity,
independence and arrogance of the Pathan; the nepotistic
network of power; the antipathy of one racial group for
another; the 'Inshallah' complex which keeps so many men
rooted like plants in the *chai khanas*; the fierce summers and
the savage winters which reduce living almost to a matter of
survival; the dream of 'Pushtunistan'.

Whether the country's ethnic ingredients can form a stable
compound, or at least a society with a controlled rate of
beneficial change, depends on a number of factors: the ability
of Afghanistan's different peoples to live and work peaceably
together on terms of equality; a steady improvement in living
standards, which in turn depends on adequate capital for
development; the growth of literacy and the rapid expansion
of technical education; the successful replacement of autocracy by democracy; the emergence of a leader of real stature
in this new political context; and the willingness of the great
powers to exercise self-restraint as well as to give material help.

135

Afghanistan

The unity of the people of Afghanistan depends very largely on the political, social and economic opportunities afforded to non-Pathans and on the willingness of the Pathans themselves, not only to make way for Uzbeg, Hazara and Tajik colleagues in many fields, but to moderate those aspects of their strong personal pride which strike others as arrogance. There is, it must be admitted, little evidence of such a change of heart in Afghanistan today; little recognition that for a while there needs to be a positive prejudice in favour of non-Pathans in all walks of life to iron out the present imbalance. If anything does bring disaster to Afghanistan in the next decade or so, it will more than likely stem from the failure to create an Afghan identity which is not merely synonymous with Pathan nationalism. If this problem is successfully solved, then others—like the Pushtunistan issue—will be less fraught with danger.

The economic development of Afghanistan depends very largely on the willingness of the countries of the outside world, and the Soviet Union in particular, to supply the necessary capital. Once they have got their direct trade route through to the Indian Ocean, will the Russians still consider it worth while to invest so heavily in their Afghan neighbour? Probably they will, for in the context of their struggle for the leadership of world communism under the banner of peaceful co-existence—however one likes to interpret that slogan—it is in Russia's interests to have a stable, peaceful and grateful sphere of influence across the Oxus. In any case, it is highly unlikely that the physical control of Afghanistan would be worth the effort, if in fact it were even possible. Afghanistan's position in this respect is likely to improve steadily with the development of those natural resources which will diminish its indebtedness to Russia. Moreover, even if Russian finance were to be sharply cut back, there is good reason to suspect that not only America, but West Germany and even Britain, would be willing to fill a substantial part of the gap.

The mass education at primary level and the greatly accelerated higher-education programme, which are the other essential ingredients of economic progress, entail a considerable threat to the established pattern of authority. Yet one of the most encouraging features of modern Afghanistan is that, despite some errors in tactics, the Afghan government appears willing to take this risk, to expand education rapidly for all classes and even for both sexes, and thus to replace aristocracy by meritocracy. One of the secondary consequences of the educational explosion must surely be in due course the release of the energies of Afghan women for the work of national development.

With the expansion of education is bound up the healthy development of democracy. In many ways democracy is a natural form of government in Afghanistan, where popular consent has always existed in various forms at tribal level. Democracy depends largely on just those creative differences of opinion which delight the Afghan and protect the individualism that is his hall-mark. If the Afghans can translate their *chai khana* arguments into constructive action, then the transition from one form of rule to another should be far more smooth than in many underdeveloped countries.

It will be even more effective a transition if, in the next few years, a man of the stature of Ahmad Shah or Abdurrahman emerges to give the dramatic and able leadership, so respected by Afghans, within this new and far more difficult context. Although none of the present Afghan leaders, worthy men as they are, falls into this category, there is such a reservoir of talent, ability and ambition that it is hard to think that such a leader will not eventually emerge. The risk which goes with this potentiality is that the ambitious conflicts of a number of such men, whether in or out of uniform, could rekindle the internal struggles with which Afghanistan is all too familiar, and either plunge the country into anarchic chaos or provide a very substantial excuse for outside intervention at the technically legal request of some shaky incumbent of governmental or royal office.

Afghanistan's prospects must also be seen within the context of change in the Indian subcontinent as a whole. If the separatist tendencies of East Pakistan ever reached the point of a breakaway into an independent sovereign state in

Bengal, then account would have to be taken of the effect on West Pakistan. Certainly, many problems of communication and government might disappear, but it is arguable that West Pakistan is not of itself a viable state. West Pakistan would be in an even weaker position if American aid were to be withdrawn or largely diminished as a result of Pakistan's flirtation with China—although it would have to become a far more serious affair to justify any such change of policy by the United States. In these circumstances, one might expect the Pushtunistan dispute to be aggravated to the point of open conflict, with disastrous consequences for both countries. Similarly, if war breaks out again between India and Pakistan over Kashmir, Afghanistan might miscalculatingly attempt to exploit the situation to resolve the Pushtunistan dispute.* China's imperialist ambitions have also to be taken into account in assessing the stability of the area, although it now seems unlikely that China will again be able to get away with a physical incursion into India without invoking more than an Indian riposte. In all of these circumstances, internal chaos or intervention by an outside power would be almost inescapable, to the equal detriment of all concerned, including Afghanistan.

It is possible that one or more of these situations might arise in the next few years and make the area so unstable as a whole that the effect on Afghanistan's future would be incalculable. But if, as seems the marginally more possible alternative, Russian and American diplomacy and Chinese preoccupation elsewhere secure the Indian subcontinent to the extent that it can concentrate on its basic problems of poverty, then the chances for Afghanistan to achieve political stability and economic viability are considerably improved, although the odds against it will still be heavy.

There then remains only the possibility of direct intervention by one of the world's two great powers on doctrinal political grounds. I have tried to argue that it is in Russia's

* It should be noted, however, that no such attempt was made by Afghanistan in late 1965, whatever rumours there may be about India's diplomacy at that time.

interest to keep Afghanistan as an obliging and co-operative but genuinely independent neighbour. That argument naturally depends on there being no dramatic change in the general, if uneven, trend of Soviet policy since the death of Stalin. There is no reason to suppose that any such change is imminent; but if, for reasons of international communist policy or as a result of American operations in Asia, Russia were to feel it necessary to show itself capable of a line at least as hard as China, then surely Afghanistan would be amongst the first demonstrations of such a change. Nevertheless, the general assumption must be that Russia will not try to exercise appreciably more direct influence in Afghanistan than it already does today.

America, it seems, has come a long way since the days of the Dullesian equation of neutralism with sin, and unless its commitment in Vietnam erodes its capacity for tolerance and restraint, one must again assume that American interests in Afghanistan will continue to be indirect and disinterestedly helpful.

The Germans will continue to invest and the French to make archaeological digs, and the British, one hopes, to exorcise the traumatic ghosts of their mutual past with Afghanistan and play a larger role in that country's development.

Afghanistan now has the opportunity it has needed for the past two hundred years. No longer a page or two in some other country's history, it can make its own. No longer a pawn in the Great Game played by others, the Afghans now control their own future. It remains to be seen what they make of it.

Appendices

HISTORICAL NOTE BY SIR OLAF CAROE

Mr John Griffiths' book displays admirable balance in the historical field, and it contains valuable new material on the development of contemporary Afghanistan.

As is to be expected, different writers on Afghanistan's affairs have different interpretations of certain aspects of the country's history. This is particularly the case in regard to two factors in Afghanistan's relations with British India: the first and second Afghan wars, and the Durand Line. Some have argued that the former were fought to no purpose, achieved nothing, and were futile exercises in Victorian imperialism; while the latter is often criticised—and here my interpretation differs from that of Mr Griffiths—as a casual cartographical arrangement, made without regard to tribal boundaries or allegiance. It may be useful for the reader to appraise an alternative interpretation of these two themes in Anglo-Afghan relations.

1. Whatever may be thought of Lord Auckland's and Lord Ellenborough's extravagances in the first Afghan war, or Lord Lytton's in the second, an impartial study of the political background in Central Asia at these times leads to the conclusion that the object and result of these wars was to keep the relatively young Afghan state out of the orbit of tsarist Russia and within that of India. The determination of British India to achieve this result was finally recognised by the article in the Anglo-Russian Convention of 1907 whereby, without occupation, Afghanistan was excluded from the Russian sphere of influence. Whether this result could have been achieved by diplomacy alone is a hypothesis on which no worth-while conclusion can now be reached. But those inclined to argue the matter must take into account the absorption of Tashkent, Samarkand, Kokand, Khiva and Bukhara by Russia in the course of its imperial expansion in the nineteenth century.

2. The fixing of the Durand Line was one result of the second Afghan war, which brought the Khyber Pass and the highlands around Quetta definitely within the Indian sphere. It was, and is, by no means arbitrary. It generally follows tribal boundaries, separating those tribes which go to market in Peshawar, Kohat, Bannu, Tank and Quetta from those with economic links with Khurasan, having Kabul, Ghazni and Kandahar as their market towns. Only in two cases—the Mohmands and the Wazirs—is a tribe divided. The Mohmands were always a two-headed Janus, many of the upper sections looking to Lalpura and Jalalabad rather than to Peshawar. These sections were left to the Amir of Afghanistan. (In the Mohmand case, a further offer was later made to the Afghan

government with a view to a definition of the Durand Line more in its favour, but the offer was never taken up.) As regards the Wazirs: a few Wazirs living in Birmal were left on the Afghan side of the Line, though the great bulk of the tribe remained in India.

It should be noted that Amir Abdurrahman went on record in his autobiography as having wholeheartedly approved this settlement. It is true that in the tribal troubles of 1895 and 1897 he showed a certain ambivalence, and was inclined to chuckle over British difficulties. This was in character, and only too natural; it would be churlish to impute blame for it.

In appraising the validity of the Durand Line, it should always be remembered that—long before the British or the sikhs appeared on the scene, and before the creation of the Afghan state by Ahmad Shah Abdali—the western Afghans (mainly Durranis and Ghaljis) and the eastern Afghans (such as Yusufzais, Mohmands, Bangash, Khataks, Afridis, Orakzais and so on) had pursued different alignments. The westerners had been subjects of Safavi Persia, and had in a measure become Persianised; the easterners, when they acknowledged any overlord, were subjects of the Mogul Empire of India. The Durand Line did something to stabilise a distinction that had roots both historical and economic.

One final point: tribute is due to Sardar Muhammad Hashim Khan, the brother of Nadir Shah. Hashim Khan held the post of Wazir-i-Azam (Prime Minister) during the first troublous sixteen years of the present Afghan dynasty. He was a great statesman, he stood for the highest traditions of the Afghan nobility, and he was in a true sense the founder and cornerstone of modern Afghanistan.

EXPORT AND IMPORT TABLES

EXPORTS AND IMPORTS 1957–61
(in million $)

Year ended March 20	1957–58	1958–59	1959–60	1960–61
Exports (f.o.b.)	58·9	46·4	60·4	49·9
Imports (c.i.f.)	57·5	72·8	80·9	86·8
Trade balance	1·4	− 26·4	− 20·5	− 36·9

EXPORTS AND IMPORTS 1961–65
(in million $)

Year ended March 20	1961–62	1962–63	1963–64	1964–65*
Exports (f.o.b.)	53·4	58·9	69·0	70·6
Imports (c.i.f.)	99·1	115·9	125·7	141·9
Trade balance	− 45·7	− 57·0	− 56·7	− 71·3

*Preliminary estimate.

PRINCIPAL EXPORTS 1963–64†
(in thousand $)

Fresh fruit	2,894·8
Dried fruit and nuts	11,524·0
Fresh and dried vegetables	227·3
Medicinal herbs	993·8
Cotton seed oil	3,448·7
Cotton	12,636·8
Wool	7,414·7
Karakul skins	16,833·5
Other pelts	482·7
Hides	2,166·2
Intestinal skins	1,715·4
Carpets	6,410·8
Miscellaneous	2,240·8
TOTAL	68,989·5

† Source: Eberhard Rhein and A. Ghanie Ghaussy, *Die Wirtschaftliche Entwicklung Afghanistans 1880–1965*, monograph published by C. W. Leske Verlag, Opladen 1966, for the Deutsches Orient-Institut.

INVESTMENT OUTLAY AND SOURCES, SECOND FIVE YEAR PLAN

(in million afghanis)

Agency	Total Investment	Sources of Finance		
		Budgetary revenues	*Private sector*	*Foreign assistance*
Ministry of Mines and Industries	10,475	2,595	146	7,734
Ministry of Public Works	10,116	3,223	—	6,893
Ministry of Agriculture	1,759	597	92	1,070
Ministry of Communications	371	98	—	273
Ministry of Education (including Kabul University)	2,190	187	—	2,003
Ministry of Health	537	57	—	480
Ministry of Commerce	40	—	20	20
Ministry of Finance	255	76	—	179
Helmand Valley	2,918	100	—	2,818
Department of Civil Aviation	802	86	—	716
Rural Development	54	11	—	43
Institute of Cartography	26	Negligible	—	26
Press Department	542	23	—	519
Government Monopoly Department	211	36	—	175
Silos	254	52	—	202
Municipalities	782	230	11	541
Auditing Department	21	21	—	—
TOTAL	31,353	7,392	269	23,692

CONSTITUTION OF AFGHANISTAN
PROMULGATED OCTOBER 1, 1964

PREAMBLE
In the Name of God, the Almighty and the Just

TO reorganise the national life of Afghanistan according to the require-ments of the time and on the basis of the realities of national history and culture;

TO achieve justice and equality;

TO establish political, economic and social democracy;

TO organise the functions of the State and its branches to ensure liberty and welfare of the individual and the maintenance of the general order;

TO achieve a balanced development of all phases of life in Afghanistan; and

TO form, ultimately, a prosperous and progressive society based on social co-operation and preservation of human dignity;

WE, the People of Afghanistan, conscious of the historical changes which have occurred in our life as a nation and as a part of human society, while considering the above-mentioned values to be the right of all human societies, have, under the leadership of His Majesty Muhammad Zahir Shah, the King of Afghanistan and the leader of its national life, framed this Constitution for ourselves and the generations to come.

TITLE ONE: THE STATE

Article 1. Afghanistan is a Constitutional Monarchy; an independent, unitary and indivisible state.

Sovereignty in Afghanistan belongs to the nation.

The Afghan nation is composed of all those individuals who possess the citizenship of the State of Afghanistan in accordance with the provisions of the law. The word Afghan shall apply to each such individual.

Art. 2. Islam is the sacred religion of Afghanistan. Religious rites performed by the State shall be according to the provisions of the Hanafi doctrine.

Non-Muslim citizens shall be free to perform their rituals within the limits determined by laws for public decency and public peace.

Art. 3. From amongst the languages of Afghanistan, Pushtu and Dari shall be the official languages.

Art. 4. The flag of Afghanistan is tri-colour—black, red and green—

147

all pieces joined together vertically from left to right in equal proportions; the breadth of each strip equalling half of its length, having in
the middle the insignia of the mehrab* and the member† in white,
flanked by two flags and ensconced in two sheaves of wheat.

Art. 5. The capital of Afghanistan is the city of Kabul.

TITLE TWO: THE KING

Art. 6. In Afghanistan the King personifies the sovereignty.

Art. 7. The King is the protector of the basic principles of the sacred
religion of Islam, the guardian of Afghanistan's independence and
territorial integrity, the custodian of its Constitution and the centre
of its national unity.

Art. 8. The King shall be an Afghan national, a Muslim and a follower
of the Hanafi doctrine.

Art. 9. The King has the following rights and duties:

1. Holds Supreme Command of the armed forces of Afghanistan.

2. Declares war and armistice.

3. Summons and inaugurates the Loya Jirgah.‡

4. Inaugurates the ordinary session of the Shura.§

5. Summons and inaugurates the extraordinary sessions of the
Shura.

6. Dissolves the Shura and decrees new elections, which shall
be held within three months from the date of the dissolution of
the Shura.

7. Signs laws and proclaims their enforcement.

8. Issues ordinances.

9. Grants credentials for conclusion of international treaties, in
accordance with the provisions of the law.

10. Signs international treaties.

11. Appoints the Prime Minister and accepts his resignation.
Appoints Ministers on the recommendation of the Prime Minister
and accepts their resignations.

12. Appoints the non-elected members of the Meshrano Jirgah‖
and appoints its President from amongst its members.

13. Appoints the Chief Justice and Justices of the Supreme Court.

14. Appoints Judges and high-ranking civil and military officials
and grants them retirement in accordance with the provisions of
the law.

15. Accredits the Heads of Afghanistan's diplomatic missions to
foreign States; appoints permanent Representatives of Afghanis-

* The mehrab is an arch in a Mosque where the prayer-leader stands, facing
the Kaaba in Mecca.

† The member is a many-tiered pulpit placed to the right of the mehrab in
a mosque, from which addresses are delivered.

‡ The Great Council.   § Parliament.   ‖ House of the Elders.

tan to international organisations and accepts the credentials of foreign diplomatic representatives.

16. Proclaims and ends the state of emergency.

17. Remits and pardons sentences.

Art. 10. Coin is minted in the name of the King.

Art. 11. The name of the King is mentioned in khutbas.*

Art. 12. Medals are awarded by the King in accordance with the terms of the law.

The award of medals shall not carry any material benefit.

Art. 13. The Royal expenditures shall be fixed in the State budget according to the law of the Royal Expenses.

Art. 14. The exercise of rights and duties described under this Title shall be subject to the limits prescribed by the provisions of this Constitution.

Art. 15. The King is not accountable and shall be respected by all.

He takes the following oath, in the presence of the members of the Royal family, the members of the Government and the Justices of the Supreme Court, in a joint sitting of both Houses of the Shura.

> 'In the name of God, the Great, I swear to be conscious of His Omnipresence in all my actions, that I shall protect the sacred principles of the religion of Islam, shall guard the Constitution, shall protect the independence and territorial integrity of the country as well as the laws of the State and the rights of the people; and, invoking Divine Assistance, shall reign in accordance with the provisions of the Constitution of Afghanistan and devote my efforts to the well-being and progress of the Afghan nation.'

Art. 16. The succession to the Throne of Afghanistan shall continue in the House of His Majesty Muhammad Nadir Shah, the Martyr, in accordance with the provisions of this Constitution.

Art. 17. Should the King resolve to abdicate, he shall inform a Council consisting of the President of the Wolesi Jirgah,† the President of the Meshrano Jirgah, the Prime Minister, the Chief Justice and the Minister of the Royal Court and, thereafter, convene a meeting of the Loya Jirgah within a period of seven days and announce therein his abdication in person or through the Minister of Court.

If the Loya Jirgah attests that the abdication has stemmed from the will of the King, the abdication shall be considered effective from the date of the attestation.

Art. 18. On the King's abdication or death, the Throne shall pass on to his eldest son.

If the eldest son of the King lacks the qualifications set forth in this Constitution, the Throne shall pass on to his second son and so on.

* The khutba is an address delivered as a religious rite on occasions specified in the Islamic religion.

† House of the People.

Afghanistan

Art. 19. Whenever the King abdicates or dies without a son possessing the qualifications to become the King, the Throne shall pass on to the oldest of the King's brothers.

In case the oldest of the King's brothers lacks the qualifications needed, the Throne shall pass on to the second brother in line and so on.

If the King does not have a brother possessing the qualifications required for the King, his successor shall be elected from amongst the male-lineal descendants of His Majesty Muhammad Nadir Shah, the Martyr. In this case the King shall be elected by an Electoral College consisting of the Loya Jirgah, the Government, and the Justices of the Supreme Court. This Electoral College shall be summoned by the Prime Minister, in the case of the death of the King within fifteen days from the date of the demise and in the case of abdication within seven days from the date when the King's abdication becomes effective. The decision of this Electoral College shall be by a majority of votes of the members present and shall be considered effective upon the consent of the person chosen as the King.

The Minister of Court shall act as Regent from the time of the death of the King or the validation of his abdication until the election of his successor.

Art. 20. The King shall, when he decides to travel out of the country, appoint one or more persons to act as his Regent or Regents. Such person or persons shall, during the absence of the King and on his behalf, discharge the Royal functions in accordance with the provisions of this Constitution and within the limits of the authority delegated to him or them by the King.

The following persons shall not be appointed as Regent:

1. The Prime Minister
2. The President of the Wolesi Jirgah
3. The President of the Meshrano Jirgah
4. The Chief Justice

Art. 21. In case the King dies before his successor has completed twenty years of life, the Queen shall act as Regent until his successor reaches the stipulated age.

In case the Queen be not living, the Electoral College, provided under Article 19 of this Constitution, shall elect someone from amongst the male-lineal descendants of His Majesty Muhammad Nadir Shah, the Martyr, to act as Regent.

Art. 22. Whenever the King abdicates and his successor has not completed twenty years of life, the Electoral College, provided under Article 19 shall elect someone from amongst the male-lineal descendants of His Majesty Muhammad Nadir Shah, the Martyr, to act as Regent until the successor reaches the stipulated age.

Art. 23. The Regent of the King must possess the qualifications specified in Article 8.

The Regent shall perform the royal functions in accordance with the provisions of this Constitution.

In the case of the Queen acting as Regent, the exercise of the authority described in section two of Article 9 shall take place with the advice of the Government.

The Regent, during the tenure of his office, cannot engage in any other profession.

The person elected as Regent by virtue of Articles 21 and 22 of this Constitution shall never be elected as the King of Afghanistan.

During the period of Regency, the provisions relating to succession under the Title 'King' of this Constitution shall not be amended.

Art. 24. The Royal House is composed of the sons, the daughters, the brothers and the sisters of the King and their husbands, wives, sons and daughters; and the paternal uncles and the sons of the paternal uncles of the King.

In the official protocol of the State, the Royal House comes after the King and the Queen.

The expenditure of the Royal House shall be fixed in the budget of the Royal Expenses.

Titles of nobility are exclusively confined to the Royal House and shall be assigned in accordance with the provisions of the law.

Members of the Royal House shall not participate in political parties, and shall not hold the following offices:

1. Prime Minister or Minister
2. Member of the Shura
3. Justice of the Supreme Court

Members of the Royal House shall maintain their status as members of the Royal House as long as they live.

TITLE THREE:
THE BASIC RIGHTS AND DUTIES OF THE PEOPLE

Art. 25. The people of Afghanistan, without any discrimination or preference, have equal rights and obligations before the law.

Art. 26. Liberty is the natural right of the human being. This right has no limitations except the liberty of others and public interest as defined by the law.

The liberty and dignity of the human being are inviolable and inalienable.

The State has the duty to respect and protect the liberty and dignity of the individual.

No deed is considered a crime except by virtue of a law in force before its commission.

No one may be punished except by the order of a competent court rendered after an open trial held in the presence of the accused.

No one may be punished except under the provisions of a law that has come into effect before the commission of the offence with which the accused is charged.

No one may be pursued or arrested except in accordance with the provisions of the law.

No one may be detained except on order of a competent court, in accordance with the provisions of the law.

Innocence is the original state; the accused is considered to be innocent unless found guilty by a final judgment of a court of law.

Crime is a personal deed. Pursuit, arrest or detention of the accused and the execution of sentence against him does not affect any other person.

Torturing a human being is not permissible. No one can torture or issue orders to torture a person even for the sake of discovering facts, even if the person involved is under pursuit, arrest or detention or is condemned to a sentence.

Imposing punishment incompatible with human dignity is not permissible.

A statement obtained from an accused or any other person by compulsion is not valid.

Confession of a crime means the admission made by an accused willingly and in full possession of his senses before a competent court with regard to the commission of a crime legally attributed to him. Every person has the right to appoint defence counsel for the removal of a charge legally attributed to him.

Indebtedness of one to another cannot cause deprivation or curtailment of the liberty of the debtor. The ways and means of recovering debt shall be specified in the law.

Every Afghan is entitled to travel within the territory of his State and settle anywhere except in areas prohibited by the law. Similarly, every Afghan has a right to travel outside of Afghanistan and return to Afghanistan according to the provisions of the law.

No Afghan shall be sentenced to banishment from Afghanistan or within its territory.

Art. 27. No Afghan accused of a crime can be extradited to a foreign state.

Art. 28. A person's residence is inviolable. No one, including the State, can enter or search a residence without the permission of the resident or the orders of a competent court and in accordance with the conditions and procedure specified by the law.

In cases of witnessed crimes the responsible officer can enter or search the residence of a person without the permission of the resident or the prior writ of the court on his personal responsibility. The officer is bound to get the order of the court within the time limit set by the law after his entry into the house or its search.

Art. 29. Property is inviolable.

No one's property can be confiscated except in accordance with the provision of the law and the decision of a competent court.

Expropriation is allowed only for securing public interest, against an advance equitable compensation, in accordance with the provisions of the law.

No one shall be prohibited from acquiring property and exercising the right of ownership of the same, within the limitations of the law. The ways of utilising property shall be regulated and guided by the law, for securing the public interest.

Investigations and declarations of a person's property can be made only in accordance with the provisions of the law.

Foreign States and nationals are not entitled to own immovable property in Afghanistan. Subject to the approval of the Government, immovable property may be sold to the diplomatic missions of foreign States on a reciprocal basis and also to those international organisations of which the State of Afghanistan is a member.

Art. 30. The freedom and secrecy of people's communications, whether by writing, telephone, telegraph or other medium, are inviolable.

The State has no right to search personal communications except by the order of a competent court and in accordance with the provisions of the law.

In urgent cases, defined by the law, the official responsible can search communications on his responsibility, without the prior permission of the court. The official concerned is bound to obtain, after the search, the decision of the court within the time limit set under the law.

Art. 31. Freedom of thought and expression is inviolable.

Every Afghan has the right to express his thoughts in speech, in writing, in pictures and by other means, in accordance with the provisions of the law.

Every Afghan has the right to print and publish ideas in accordance with the provisions of the law, without submission in advance to the authorities of the State.

The permission to establish and own public printing houses and to issue publications is granted only to the citizens and the State of Afghanistan, in accordance with the provisions of the law.

The establishment and operation of public radio transmission and telecasting is the exclusive right of the State.

Art. 32. Afghan citizens have the right to assemble unarmed, without prior permission of the State, for the achievement of legitimate and peaceful purposes, in accordance with the provisions of the law.

Afghan citizens have the right to establish, in accordance with the provisions of the law, associations for the realisation of material or spiritual purposes.

Afghan citizens have the right to form political parties, in accordance with the terms of the law, provided that:

Afghanistan

1. The aims and activities of the party and the ideas on which the organisation of the party is based are not opposed to the values embodied in this Constitution.

2. The organisation and financial resources of the party are open.

A party formed in accordance with the provisions of the law cannot be dissolved without due process of the law and the order of the Supreme Court.

Art. 33. Anyone who, without due cause, suffers damage from the Administration is entitled to compensation and may file a suit in a court for its recovery.

The State cannot, except in cases specified by the law, resort to the recovery of its dues without the order of a competent court.

Art. 34. Education is the right of every Afghan and shall be provided free of charge by the State and the citizens of Afghanistan. The aim of the State in this sphere is to reach a stage where suitable facilities for education will be made available to all Afghans, in accordance with the provisions of the law. The Government is obliged to prepare and implement a programme for balanced and universal education in Afghanistan.

It is the duty of the State to guide and supervise education.

Primary education is compulsory for all children in areas where facilities for this purpose are provided by the State.

The State alone has the right and duty to establish and administer the institutions of public and higher learning. Outside this sphere, Afghan nationals are entitled to establish technical and literacy schools. Conditions for the establishment of such schools, their curricula and the conditions of learning in such schools are to be determined by law.

The Government may grant permission, in accordance with the provisions of the law, to foreign persons to establish private schools for the exclusive use of foreigners.

Art. 35. It is the duty of the State to prepare and implement an effective programme for the development and strengthening of the national language, Pushtu.

Art. 36. It is the duty of the State to provide, within the limits of its means, balanced facilities for the prevention and treatment of diseases for all Afghans. The aim of the State in this respect is to reach a stage where suitable medical facilities will be made available to all Afghans.

Art. 37. Work is the right and precept of every Afghan who has the capability to do it.

The main purpose of laws designed to systematise labour is to reach a stage where the rights and interests of all categories of labourers are protected, suitable conditions of work are provided and the relations between the workers and employers are organised on a just and progressive basis.

The citizens of Afghanistan are admitted to the service of the State

Appendices

on the basis of their qualifications and in accordance with the provisions of the law.

Work and trade may be freely chosen, within the conditions determined by the law.

Forced labour even for the benefit of the State is not permissible. The prohibition of forced labour shall not be so construed as to affect the implementation of the laws governing the organisation of collective work for the public interest.

Art. 38. Every Afghan is bound to pay tax and duty to the State. No duty or tax of any kind shall be levied without the provisions of the law. The rate of tax and duty as well as the method of payment shall be determined by law with consideration for social justice. The provisions of this Article are applicable to foreign persons as well.

Art. 39. It is the sacred duty of all citizens of Afghanistan to defend their country. All citizens of Afghanistan are bound to perform military service in accordance with the provisions of the law.

Art. 40. It is the duty of all the people of Afghanistan to follow the provisions of the Constitution; to bear loyalty to the King and respect him; to obey laws; to have due consideration for public order and peace; to protect the interests of the homeland and to participate in the national life.

TITLE FOUR: THE SHURA

Art. 41. The Shura in Afghanistan manifests the will of the people and represents the whole of the nation.

The people of Afghanistan participate through the Shura in the political life of the country. Although elected from a particular constituency each member of the Shura shall at the time of expressing his opinion take the general interest of the whole of Afghanistan as the basis for his judgment.

Art. 42. The Shura consists of two houses:

Wolesi Jirgah

Meshrano Jirgah

Art. 43. Members of the Wolesi Jirgah shall be elected by the people of Afghanistan in a free, universal, secret and direct election, in accordance with the provisions of the law. For this purpose Afghanistan shall be divided into electoral constituencies, the number and limits of which are fixed by the law. Each constituency shall return one member. The candidate who obtains the largest number of votes cast in his constituency, in accordance with the provisions of the law, shall be recognised as the representative of that constituency.

Art. 44. Members of the Wolesi Jirgah shall be elected for a period of four years, which is one term of the legislature. Whenever the Shura is dissolved, in accordance with the provisions of this constitution, a new Wolesi Jirgah shall be elected for another legislative term. However, the termination date of the outgoing House is so regulated that the ensuing session of the Wolesi Jirgah commences on the date stipulated in Article 59.

Art. 45. Members of the Meshrano Jirgah shall be nominated and elected as follows:

1. One third of the members shall be appointed by the King for a period of five years from amongst well-informed and experienced persons.

2. The remaining two-thirds of the members shall be elected as follows:

a. Each Provincial Council shall elect one of its members to the Meshrano Jirgah for a period of three years.

b. The residents of each province shall elect one person for a period of four years by a free, universal, secret and direct election.

Art. 46. Qualifications for voters shall be specified in the electoral law.

Persons appointed or elected for membership in the Shura must meet the following requirements in addition to their qualifications as voters:

1. Must have acquired Afghan nationality at least ten years prior to the date of nomination or election.

2. Must not have been punished by a court with deprivation of political rights after the promulgation of this constitution.

3. Must be able to read and write.

4. Members of the Wolesi Jirgah must have completed the age of 25 at the time of the election and those of the Meshrano Jirgah the age of 30 at the time of their nomination or election.

Art. 47. The Head and members of the government, Judges, officers and members of the armed forces, officials and other personnel of the administration cannot be appointed or elected to the Shura while they are in service.

Art. 48. No person can be a member of both Houses simultaneously.

Art. 49. Elections shall be governed by the electoral law subject to the provisions of this Constitution.

No bill to amend the electoral law may be entertained on the agenda of either house of the Shura during the last two years of the legislative term of the Wolesi Jirgah.

Art. 50. Documents of membership are authenticated in each House by the House itself. The procedure of authentication shall be specified in the rules of procedure of the House concerned.

Art. 51. No legal proceedings can be brought against a member of the Shura for expressing an opinion or idea while performing his duty inside or outside the Shura.

Whenever a member of the Shura is accused of an offence, the official responsible shall communicate the matter to the House of which the accused is a member. The legal proceedings against the accused shall be initiated when the House votes its approval by a two-thirds majority of its members. The House can also rescind its permission by a two-thirds majority vote of its members.

In the case of a witnessed crime the official responsible can start legal proceedings and arrest a member of the Shura without the permission of the House to which he belongs.

Whenever legal proceedings demand the detention of the accused in accordance with the provisions of the law, the official responsible is bound to communicate the matter immediately to the House concerned, and with its permission may detain the accused. In case the accusation occurs during the period when the House is not in session, permission for detention shall be obtained from the Executive Council of the House. The decision of the Executive Council shall be placed before the House at its next session for appropriate action.

Art. 52. Members of the Shura cannot undertake any other profession. This rule does not apply to agriculture and other free enterprises.

Art. 53. Suitable salaries shall be fixed in accordance with the law for members of Shura.

Art. 54. Every member of Shura is entitled to express his views on the subject of debate in his House, in accordance with the Rules of Procedure.

Art. 55. The two Houses meet separately but at the same time.

The Meshrano Jirgah can hold extraordinary sessions to study the budget proposals of the State during the time when the Wolesi Jirgah is adjourned.

A joint session of the two Houses of Shura is held when the King inaugurates the new Shura or addresses the annual session of the Shura.

Art. 56. The members of the Government may attend the meetings of both Houses of Shura.

Each House may demand the presence of the Head or members of the Government at its meetings.

Art. 57. Debates in both Houses are open except when the Government, the President of the House or at least ten members request a secret session, and the House grants its approval. The House can, with a two-thirds majority of the members, convert secret proceedings into open debate.

The proceedings of both Houses of Shura are recorded.

Nobody may enter the meeting place of the Shura by force. Violators shall be punished according to the law.

Art. 58. Except in cases clearly defined in this Constitution, decisions in each House shall be made by a majority vote of the members present.

Art. 59. Each House of Shura holds one ordinary session per year, which opens on the 22nd of Meezan. The number of annual sessions can be increased by law. In such cases the law shall regulate the opening date of the session and its duration.

The working period of each House of Shura is seven months per year. This period may be extended by each House according to the requirements of its business.

During the recess period, an extraordinary session of Shura may be summoned by the King; or on a request by the Government, the President of one of the Houses, or by one-fifth of its members.

The extraordinary session of Shura ends by a Royal Decree issued after consultation with the Presidents of both Houses.

Art. 60. The President of the Meshrano Jirgah is appointed from amongst its members by the King.

The Wolesi Jirgah elects one of its members as President of the House.

Each House elects from amongst its members one First Deputy President, one Second Deputy President, one Secretary and one Deputy Secretary. The above mentioned persons constitute the Executive Council of the House.

The Executive Council of the Wolesi Jirgah is elected at the opening of the legislative term while the Vice-Presidents, Secretary and Deputy Secretary of the Meshrano Jirgah are elected for one year at the beginning of each annual session.

The President of each House conducts debates in the House concerned and adopts necessary measures for the maintenance of law and order on the premises of the House. Other duties of the President are defined in the Rules of Procedure for the House. In the absence of the President, the First Deputy President, and in the absence of the First Deputy President, the Second Deputy President officiates as President.

The Secretary of the House records the proceedings of the House and supervises the functions of its Secretariat. In the absence of the Secretary the Deputy Secretary discharges the duties of the Secretary.

Art. 61. Each House appoints, in accordance with its Rules of Procedure, committees for making thorough and detailed study of the subjects under consideration.

Art. 62. Each House formulates its own Rules of Procedure.

Art. 63. The Shura may be dissolved by order of the King.

The dissolution of the Shura is imperative under the conditions described in Article 121.

The dissolution of the Shura encompasses the non-elected members of the Meshrano Jirgah.

Art. 64. The Shura legislates for organising the affairs of the country in accordance with the provisions of this Constitution.

There shall be no law repugnant to the basic principles of the sacred religion of Islam and the other values embodied in this Constitution.

The ratification of international treaties, the dispatch abroad of detachments of Afghan armed forces, the grant of concessions important to the national economy including monopolies, and the authorisation to issue money and obtain loans are within the competence of the Shura. Concessions which are to be ratified by the Shura shall be defined by the law.

Art. 65. The Government is responsible to the Wolesi Jirgah.

Art. 66. The members of the Wolesi Jirgah may put questions to the Government. Debate on the Government explanation depends upon the decision of the House.

Art. 67. The members of the Shura may ask questions from the Prime Minister or the Ministers about specific subjects.

Persons thus asked are bound to furnish a verbal or written answer. This answer shall not be made subject of debate.

Art. 68. The Wolesi Jirgah is competent to appoint, on proposal from one-third of its members, an Enquiry Commission to investigate and study the conduct of the Government and the actions of the administration. The composition of the Enquiry Commission and its method of functioning shall be defined in the Rules of Procedure of the House.

Art. 69. Excepting the conditions for which specific provisions have been made in this Constitution, a law is a resolution passed by both Houses, and signed by the King. In the area where no such law exists, the provisions of the Hanafi Jurisprudence of the Sharia'at of Islam shall be considered as law.

Art. 70. A legislative bill may be introduced to the Shura by the Government or the members of the Shura. Bills relating to Judicial administration may also be introduced by the Supreme Court. Bills relating to budgetary and financial legislation may only originate from the Government.

Art. 71. A legislative bill may be introduced to either of the two Houses by the Government or the Supreme Court.

Art. 72. When a bill is introduced by members of one of the two Houses, it is placed on the agenda of the House only after it is supported by at least ten members of the House concerned.

A bill which involves new financial commitments or a reduction in state revenue may be placed on the agenda of either House on condition that the bill provides for the sources of financing for the compensation of the loss. This provision does not apply to bills introduced by the Supreme Court.

Art. 73. When a bill is placed on the agenda of either of the two Houses, it is first referred to the committee concerned, and after it has been commented upon by the committee, the bill is read in the House along with the comments of the committee, and debated upon, followed by voting on each article. After this the draft is read for the second time and put before the House for rejection or approval as a whole.

Art. 74. When an enactment of one House is rejected by the other, a joint committee consisting of an equal number of members from both Houses is set up, in accordance with the provisions of the law, to settle the differences. The verdict of the committee becomes effective after it receives the Royal Assent. When the joint committee fails to resolve the differences, the enactment is considered invalid. If the enactment is from the Wolesi Jirgah, it may be approved again by a majority of votes during the next term of legislation. The enactment, without reference to the Meshrano Jirgah, then becomes law after it is signed by the King.

When the differences between the two Houses of the Shura relate to financial bills and are not resolved by the joint committee, the Wolesi Jirgah may move the bill again in the following session and approve it by a majority vote. This enactment, without reference to the Meshrano Jirgah, becomes law after it is signed by the King.

Art. 75. The State budget is presented to the Wolesi Jirgah through the Meshrano Jirgah together with their advisory comments.

The President of the Wolesi Jirgah refers the budget proposal, along with the comments of the Meshrano Jirgah, to the committee concerned. Afterwards, the budget proposal, together with the comments of the Meshrano Jirgah and of the committee concerned, are presented to the House for consideration and decision. This decision is not submitted to the Meshrano Jirgah and becomes effective after it is signed by the King. This provision also applies to discussions on the development plans of the Government in the Wolesi Jirgah.

Whenever for any reason the passage of the budget does not materialise before the beginning of the new fiscal year, the budget of the previous year is applicable until the new budget is adopted.

The Government is bound to submit to the Wolesi Jirgah final accounts of the budget of the previous year at least one month before the submission of the new budget.

Art. 76. When the Meshrano Jirgah does not give its decision on an enactment referred to it by the Wolesi Jirgah within six months from the date of its receipt, the enactment is considered to have been adopted. In calculating this time, the period of adjournment is not taken into account.

Art. 77. During adjournment or dissolution of the Shura the Government may formulate ordinances for regulating urgent matters in respect to paragraph one of Article 64. These ordinances shall become law after being signed by the King. The ordinances shall be submitted to the Shura within thirty days of the first meeting of the Shura. If rejected the ordinances shall become invalid.

TITLE FIVE: THE LOYA JIRGAH

Art. 78. The Loya Jirgah consists of members of the Shura and the Chairmen of the Provincial Councils.

In the event of the dissolution of the Shura its members retain their position as members of the Loya Jirgah until a new Shura comes into being.

Art. 79. Subject to the provisions of Articles 19, 21 and 22 of this Constitution, the Loya Jirgah is summoned by a Royal proclamation.

Art. 80. When the Loya Jirgah is in session, the provisions of Article 51 are applicable to its members.

Art. 81. The deliberations of the Loya Jirgah are open unless the Government or at least twenty members of the Loya Jirgah request a secret session and the Loya Jirgah approves this request.

Art. 82. The President of the Wolesi Jirgah, and, in his absence, the President of the Meshrano Jirgah presides over the Loya Jirgah.

The Loya Jirgah, at its first meeting, elects one of its members as Secretary.

Art. 83. Except in cases clearly defined in this Constitution, the decisions of the Loya Jirgah shall be by a majority of the votes of its members present.

The procedure of the Loya Jirgah shall be regulated by law, subject to the provisions of this Constitution.

Art. 84. The Loya Jirgah enjoys the powers defined in this Constitution.

TITLE SIX: THE GOVERNMENT

Art. 85. The Government of Afghanistan consists of the Prime Minister and the Ministers. The Prime Minister is the Head and the Ministers are the members of the Government. The number of Ministers and their functions shall be regulated by law.

Art. 86. Any person who, in accordance with the provisions of this Constitution, is eligible for election to the Wolesi Jirgah may be appointed as the Head or member of the Government.

The Head of the Government shall be an Afghan by birth. The Head and members of the Government may be appointed from the members of the Shura or outside of it. Any member of the Shura appointed as the Head or a member of the Government shall cease to be a member of the Shura.

Art. 87. The Prime Minister and the Ministers cannot engage in any other profession during their tenure of office.

Art. 88. Suitable salaries shall be fixed by law for the Head and members of the Government.

Art. 89. The Government shall be formed by the person designated as Prime Minister by the King.

The members and policy of the Government are presented by the Prime Minister to the Wolesi Jirgah, which, after debate, resolves on a vote of confidence in the Government. When the vote of confidence is given, the King issues a Royal decree appointing the Head and members of the Government.

Afterwards the Prime Minister acquaints the Meshrano Jirgah with the policy of the Government.

Art. 90. Whenever a Government falls because of the death or resignation of the Prime Minister during the dissolution of the Shura, a new Government shall be appointed by a Royal decree. The Prime Minister shall introduce the members of the Government and its policy to the Wolesi Jirgah at the opening of the new term of Shura and shall ask for a vote of confidence.

Art. 91. The Government falls in the following circumstances:

1. On the Prime Minister's resignation or death.

2. On a vote of no-confidence against the Government by the Wolesi Jirgah.

3. On the charge of high treason against the Head or all members of the Government, as stipulated in Article 93.

4. On the dissolution of the Shura.

5. On the termination of the legislative term.

In the last two cases, the Government shall cease to exist with the first meeting of the new Wolesi Jirgah.

In the case of resignation of the Prime Minister, the Government ceases to exist after the acceptance of the resignation by the King.

In the event of the Prime Minister's death, one of the Ministers, on orders from the King, discharges the duties of Prime Minister until a new Government is formed.

When the Government falls due to the allegation of high treason, under the provision of Article 93, the person appointed by the King as the Prime Minister can continue his duties without receiving a vote of confidence until the first meeting of the Wolesi Jirgah following the decision of the Loya Jirgah on the allegation.

In all other cases the outgoing Government shall continue in office until a new Government is formed.

Art. 92. The vote of no-confidence against the Government shall be specific and direct. In the two legislative terms following the promulgation of this Constitution, a vote of no-confidence against the Government shall be by a two-thirds majority of the Wolesi Jirgah and for Governments after that period, by a majority vote of the members.

Art. 93. When more than one-third of the members of the Wolesi Jirgah demand the impeachment of the Prime Minister or of a majority of the members of the Government on a charge of high treason, and the Wolesi Jirgah approves this demand by a two-thirds majority of the members, the Government falls and a meeting of the Loya Jirgah is called to appoint an Enquiry Commission. If after studying the report of the Commission, the Loya Jirgah decides by a two-thirds majority vote of the members that prosecution is necessary, it commissions a member of the Wolesi Jirgah to file a suit against the accused in the Supreme Court.

The above provision shall also apply to one or a few Ministers numbering less than half who are accused of high treason. As a result of the accusation, the accused shall be relieved of his duties but the Government shall not fall.

Art. 94. Implementation of the provisions of this Constitution and all the laws, enforcement of the final judgments of the courts, adoption of necessary measures for the maintenance of public order and security, regulation of financial affairs of the State, protection of public property, development of the social, cultural and economic condition of the people, preservation of independence, defence of territorial integrity and protection of the interests and prestige of Afghanistan in the international community are the duties of the Government.

To regulate its functions, the Government shall make Regulations based on laws. No Regulation shall be repugnant to the letter or spirit of any law.

Art. 95. The Council of Ministers lays down the basic lines of the policy of the Government and approves those regulations which are within the competence of the Government.

The Prime Minister presides over the Council of Ministers, directs and guides the activities of the Government and secures co-ordination in its work.

The Prime Minister is also responsible for maintaining liaison between the Government, on the one side, and the King and the Shura on the other side.

The Ministers discharge their duties, as heads of the administrative units, and as members of the Government, under the order and guidance of the Prime Minister within the limitations established by this Constitution and the laws.

Art. 96. The Prime Minister and the Ministers are collectively responsible to the Wolesi Jirgah for the general policy of the Government, and individually for their prescribed duties.

The Prime Minister and the Ministers are also responsible for those actions of the Government concerning which they obtain a Royal decree, in accordance with the provisions of this Constitution.

TITLE SEVEN: THE JUDICIARY

Art. 97. The Judiciary is an independent organ of the State and discharges its duties side by side with the Legislative and Executive Organs.

Art. 98. The Judiciary consists of a Supreme Court and other courts, the number of which shall be determined by law.

It is within the jurisdiction of the Judiciary to adjudicate in all litigation brought before it according to the rules of law, in which real

163

or legal persons, including the State, are involved either as plaintiff or defendant.

Under no circumstances shall a law exclude from the jurisdiction of the Judiciary, as defined in this Title, a case or sphere, and assign it to other authorities. This provision does not prevent the establishment of military courts; but the jurisdiction of these courts is confined to offences related to the armed forces of Afghanistan. The organisation and jurisdiction of the military courts shall be determined by law.

Art. 99. The judges are appointed by the King on the recommendation of the Chief Justice. Whenever a judge commits an offence, the Supreme Court considers the case of the judge, and after hearing the defence of the judge can recommend his dismissal to the King. In case the recommendation is approved by the King, the judge is dismissed from office. Transfers, promotions, calling to account, and recommendations for retirement of the judges are within the competence of the Supreme Court, in accordance with the provisions of the law.

Suitable salaries for the judges are fixed by law.

Judges cannot engage in other occupations during their tenure of office.

Art. 100. In the courts of Afghanistan trials are held openly and everyone may attend in accordance with the provisions of the law. The Court may in exceptional cases specified in the law hold closed trials. However, the judgment shall always be openly proclaimed.

The courts are bound to state in their judgments the reasons for their verdicts.

Art. 101. The enforcement of all final judgments of the courts is obligatory except in the case of a death sentence where the execution of the court decision is subject to the King's signature.

Art. 102. The courts in the cases under their consideration shall apply the provisions of this Constitution and the laws of the State. Whenever no provision exists in the Constitution or the laws for a case under consideration, the courts shall, by following the basic principles of the Hanafi Jurisprudence of the Sharia'at of Islam and within the limitations set forth in this Constitution, render a decision that in their opinion secures justice in the best possible way.

Art. 103. Investigation of crimes shall be conducted, in accordance with the provisions of the law, by the Attorney-General, who is a part of the Executive organ of the State.

Art. 104. Subject to the provisions of this Constitution, rules relating to the organisation and the function of the courts, and matters concerning judges shall be regulated by law.

The principal aim of these laws shall be the establishment of uniformity in judicial practice, organisation, jurisdiction, and procedures of the courts.

Art. 105. The Supreme Court consists of nine Judges appointed by the King.

The King shall appoint the members of the Supreme Court from amongst persons who shall:

1. Have completed 35 years.
2. Be eligible for election to the Shura in accordance with the provisions of Article 46.
3. Have sufficient knowledge of jurisprudence, the national objectives, and the laws and legal system in Afghanistan.

The King appoints one of the Judges of the Supreme Court, whose age is not less than 40 and not over 60 years, as the Chief Justice.

The King can review the appointment of the Chief Justice and the Judges of the Supreme Court after the lapse of ten years from the date of their appointment to the said offices. Subject to the provisions of this Article and of Article 106, the Chief Justice and Judges of the Supreme Court shall not be removed from their offices by any other means.

Except in the case mentioned in Article 106, the Chief Justice and Judges of the Supreme Court shall, after their tenure in office, enjoy for the rest of their lives all the financial privileges pertaining to the term of their services.

The Chief Justice and Judges of the Supreme Court shall not, after the termination of their services, become Prime Minister or members of the Government, members of the Shura or Government officials.

The Chief Justice and members of the Supreme Court shall not participate in political parties during or after their tenure of office.

Art. 106. Should more than one-third of the members of the Wolesi Jirgah demand the impeachment of the Chief Justice or one or more Judges of the Supreme Court on a charge of a crime stemming from the performance of their duties, and the Wolesi Jirgah approve this demand by a majority of two-thirds of its members, the accused is suspended from office and a meeting of the Loya Jirgah is called to appoint a Commission of Enquiry.

If the Loya Jirgah, after studying the report of the Commission, decides by a two-thirds majority of its members that the prosecution of the accused is necessary, it shall appoint one of its members to file a suit and shall appoint a panel of eight persons to act as a tribunal. The tribunal, presided over by the President of the Meshrano Jirgah, shall try the accused in accordance with the criminal procedures of the Supreme Court. The accused, if proved guilty, shall be dismissed from office and punished.

Art. 107. The Supreme Court is the highest judicial authority in Afghanistan.

The Supreme Court regulates the organisation and functions of the courts and the judicial affairs of the State in accordance with the provisions of this Constitution and the law.

Afghanistan

The Supreme Court adopts necessary measures to organise the administrative affairs of the courts.

The budget of the Judiciary is prepared by the Chief Justice in consultation with the Government and, after the approval of the Supreme Court, is presented by the Government to the Shura as a part of the State budget.

The Supreme Court administers the budget of the Judiciary.

The provisions of the law relating to civil servants and other administrative employees of the State are applicable to the civil servants and other administrative employees of the Judiciary. However, their appointment, promotion, dismissal, retirement, and calling to account shall be within the competence of the Supreme Court, in accordance with the law.

TITLE EIGHT: THE ADMINISTRATION

Art. 108. The administration of Afghanistan is based upon the principle of centralisation, in accordance with the provisions of this Title.

The Central Administration shall be divided into a number of administrative units each headed by a Minister, as provided in the law.

The unit of local administration is the province. The number, area, sub-divisions and organisation of the provinces shall be fixed by law.

Art. 109. In each province a Provincial Council shall be formed.

The members of the Provincial Council shall be elected by the residents of the province in a free, universal, direct and secret election.

The Provincial Council shall elect one of its members as Chairman.

The Provincial Councils shall take part in the realisation of the development targets of the State in the manner specified by law.

Similarly, the Provincial Councils shall advise the Provincial Government on matters pertaining to the betterment of the condition and the general development of the province.

The Provincial Council shall discharge its duties in co-operation with the Provincial Government.

Suitable salaries for the members of the Provincial Councils shall be fixed by law.

Art. 110. Laws shall be framed in accordance with the principles of this Title to organise the work of the local administration. One of the objectives of these laws shall be the extension of the councils to the village level and their ever-increasing participation in the local administration.

Art. 111. Municipalities shall be organised to administer the affairs of the cities. Municipal Councils shall be established by free, universal, direct and secret election. Subject to the provisions of this Title, matters relating to the municipalities shall be regulated by law.

Appendices

Art. 112. The functions of the administration shall be carried out by the civil servants and other administrative employees.

Suitable salaries shall be fixed by law for the civil servants and other administrative employees.

The rights and duties of the civil servants and other administrative employees shall be regulated by law.

Title Nine: State of Emergency

Art. 113. Whenever the preservation of independence and the continuance of national life become impossible through the channels provided for in this Constitution due to war, danger of war, serious disturbances, or similar conditions which endanger the country, a state of emergency shall be declared by the King.

Should a state of emergency continue for more than three months, the concurrence of the Loya Jirgah is imperative for its extension.

Art. 114. In a state of emergency, the King may transfer all or part of the powers of the Shura to the Government.

Art. 115. In a state of emergency, the Government, after obtaining the concurrence of the Supreme Court, may, by ordinances, suspend or impose restrictions upon the following provisions of this Constitution:

1. Section one of Article 28.
2. Section three of Article 29.
3. Section two of Article 30.
4. Section one of Article 32.
5. Section one of Article 33.

Art. 116. The King may, in a state of emergency, transfer the capital temporarily from the city of Kabul to another place.

Art. 117. Should the legislative term of the Wolesi Jirgah or the term of office of a part of the members of the Meshrano Jirgah come to an end during the state of emergency, the king may postpone the holding of new elections and extend the legislative term of the Wolesi Jirgah or the term of office of the said members of the Meshrano Jirgah, until the state of emergency comes to an end. Elections shall be held immediately after the termination of the state of emergency.

Art. 118. The Constitution shall not be amended during a state of emergency.

Art. 119. At the end of a state of emergency, the measures adopted under Article 115 become immediately invalid.

Measures adopted by the Government in accordance with the provisions of Article 114 shall be submitted to the Shura within one month from the date of its first meeting following the end of the state of emergency. These measures become null and void if the Shura rejects them.

Whenever during a state of emergency a Government has been formed which has not obtained a vote of confidence from the Wolesi Jirgah

Afghanistan

under the provision of Article 114, a motion for a vote of confidence shall be put immediately before the Wolesi Jirgah after the end of the state of emergency, for debate and decision thereon.

Title Ten: Amendment

Art. 120. Adherence to the basic principles of Islam, Constitutional Monarchy in accordance with the provisions of this Constitution, and the values embodied in Article 8 shall not be subject to amendment.

Amendments to other provisions of the Constitution may be initiated by the Council of Ministers or one-third of the members of the Wolesi Jirgah or the Meshrano Jirgah, in accordance with the provisions of this Title.

Art. 121. The proposal for amendment is discussed by the Loya Jirgah, and in case a majority of the members approves its necessity, a committee from amongst its members shall be appointed to formulate the amendment. The committee shall formulate the amendment with the advice of the Council of Ministers and the Supreme Court, for submission to the Loya Jirgah. In case the Loya Jirgah approves the draft amendment with a majority vote of its members, it is submitted to the King. The King shall dissolve the Shura, circulate the draft amendment to the public and proclaim the date of the new elections. The new elections shall take place within four months from the dissolution of the Shura.

Art. 122. Following the opening of the Shura and the formation of the Government the King summons the Loya Jirgah, which, after consideration, approves or rejects the text of the draft amendment. The decision of the Loya Jirgah in this respect shall be by a two-thirds majority vote of its members and shall be enforced after it has been signed by the King.

Title Eleven: Transitional Provisions

Art. 123. Subject to the provisions of this Title, this Constitution shall come into force from the date it is signed and proclaimed by the King.

Art. 124. After the King proclaims this Constitution, the National Assembly and the Senate are considered to be dissolved.

Art. 125. The new Shura shall be inaugurated on Meezan 22, 1344, AH.*

The period between the proclamation of this Constitution and the inauguration of the new Shura shall be considered the Interim Period.

During the Interim Period, the powers of the Shura are transferred to the Government.

Ordinances issued during the Interim Period, under the provisions

* i.e. October 14, 1965.

of this Title, shall be submitted to the Wolesi Jirgah in accordance with the provisions of Article 77.

If during the Interim Period a situation arises, which, in accordance with the provisions of this Constitution, necessitates the convening of the Loya Jirgah, the dissolved National Assembly and the Senate shall be summoned and the Loya Jirgah constituted in accordance with the provisions of Article 78.

If the Provincial Councils are not in existence when one of the above-mentioned situations arises, the Loya Jirgah shall be constituted without the Chairmen of the Provincial Councils.

Art. 126. The following shall be among the duties of the Government during the Interim Period:

1. To prepare ordinances relating to elections, basic organisation of the State, the press, and judicial organisation and jurisdiction, and to submit the same to the King for his signature.

2. To prepare drafts of bills relating to political parties and Provincial Councils, and to submit them to the Shura, convened after the Interim Period.

3. To adopt necessary measures and prepare the ground for the implementation of the provisions of this Constitution.

Art. 127. The Supreme Court shall come into existence on the 22nd day of Meezan, 1346 AH.* If in the interim the applications of the provisions of Articles 15, 17, 19, 21, 22, and 115 of this Constitution is called for, the provisions of the said Articles shall be enforced without the participation of the Supreme Court or the Chief Justice.

During the time between the proclamation of this Constitution and the establishment of the Supreme Court, the King has the authority to take necessary measures for securing the performance of the functions of the Supreme Court.

Art. 128. Laws, issued prior to the proclamation of this Constitution shall be considered effective provided they are not repugnant to the provisions of this Constitution and are not nullified by new laws.

* i.e. October 14, 1967.

References

1. The Pivot of Fortune

1. Sir W. Fraser-Tytler, *Afghanistan*, Oxford University Press, London and New York, 2nd edn 1953, p. 28.
2. *Baburnama*, p. 136. Babur's account of his life seems to have experienced almost as many vicissitudes as its author. The narrative is frequently broken off, leaving exasperatingly intriguing gaps—caused, doubtless, by the more immediate necessities of his hazardous life. Fortunately, several copies of the original Chagatai Turki were made in Persian, and the main thread of Babur's endearingly honest account of his life and loves, wars and wine-drinking is thus preserved. Quotations from it in the text are adapted from the translation by John Leyden and William Erskine (London 1826), to which the page numbers refer. Annette Beveridge's translation (*Babar, Emperor of Hindustan: The Babar-Nama*, fasc. 4 vols, London 1912-21) is more scholarly but was not available for consultation.

3. *Baburnama*, p. 138.
4. Cited in Fraser-Tytler, *op. cit.*, p. 50.
5. Mountstuart Elphinstone, *Account of the Kingdom of Caubul*, London 1815.

2. The Great Game

1. John McNeill to Lord Palmerston, April 11, 1838: *Correspondence Relating to Persia and Afghanistan*, printed for Her Majesty's Government by J. Harrison and Son, London 1839. Cited in Fraser-Tytler, *op. cit.*, p. 100.
2. Cited in Fraser-Tytler, *op. cit.*, p. 104.
3. Sir Thomas Holdich, *The Indian Borderland*, Methuen, London 1901, pp. 366, 371.
4. Cited in Fraser-Tytler, *op. cit.*, p. 319.
5. *Ibid.*, p. 138.
6. Cited in John Morley, *Life of Gladstone*, Macmillan, London, 1906 edn, Vol. II, p. 203.
7. Cited in Fraser-Tytler, *op. cit.*, p. 153.
8. Holdich, *op. cit.*, p. 50.
9. Cited in R. I. Bruce, *The Forward Policy and its Results*, London 1900, p. 347.

References

10. Hansard, House of Lords Debates, March 7, 1898.
11. *Memoirs of Count Pahlen* (trans. N. J. Couriss), Oxford University Press, London and New York 1964.

4. 'Pushtunistan Unjast'

1. James Thomson, *The Seasons*: 'Summer', 1727 edition.
2. Elphinstone, *op. cit.*, p. 253.

Short Reading List

For a general historical background, there is no more readable and stimulating book than *The Pathans* by Sir Olaf Caroe (Macmillan, London; St Martin's Press, New York; 2nd edn 1962). Although it excludes some aspects of Afghan history it has the particular merit of giving the background of the Pathans in Pakistan. For a broader but thorough history, Sir William Fraser-Tytler's *Afghanistan* (Oxford University Press, London and New York, 2nd edn 1953) is among the more recent and best. Less valuable, but useful as a counterweight to British writers, is the American Arnold Fletcher's *Afghanistan: Highway of Conquest* (Cornell University Press, Ithaca, N.Y., 1965).

For history written as it took place, Mountstuart Elphinstone's *Account of the Kingdom of Caubul* (London 1815) and *The Indian Borderland* by Sir Thomas Holdich (London 1901) can be recommended; while an Afghan viewpoint emerges clearly, if not always frankly, from *The Life of Abdurrahman, Amir of Afghanistan*, edited by Mir Munshi Sultan Mohammed Khan (London 1900).

A most graphic account of modern Afghanistan can be found in Andrew Wilson's *North from Kabul* (Allen and Unwin, London 1961), while Peter Mayne writes with considerable artistry of the Pathans as a whole in *The Narrow Smile* (Murray, London 1955). For an admirable impression of the 'atmosphere' of the area, there is Eric Newby's *A Short Walk in the Hindu Kush* (Secker and Warburg, London 1958).

Authoritative information on the structure and *mores* of the country's inhabitants is given in Donald N. Wilber (ed.), *Afghanistan: Its People, Its Society, Its Culture* (Human Relations Area Files, New Haven, Conn., 1962). Wilber's *Annotated Bibliography of Afghanistan* (Human Relations Area Files, New Haven, Conn., 1962) is the most complete bibliography available. The most recent work on the Afghan economy is in German: *Die Wirtschaftliche Entwicklung Afghanistans 1880–1965* by Eberhard Rhein and A. Ghanie Ghaussy (C. W. Leske Verlag, Opladen 1966).

Index

Abdali tribe, 5; *see also* Durrani tribe
Abdurrahman, Amir, 24, 30, 51–2, 137, 144
Abu Bakr, Mrs Rokyan, 82
Achaemenian rule, 8
Adija, Mrs, 82
Administrative system, 93, 95–6, 98, 105, 111*ff*., 132, 154, 166–7
Aeroflot, 39
Afghan people, 7–8, 65
Afghan wars: first (1838–42), 19, 143; second (1878–81), 22, 23, 143; third (war of Independence, 1919), 31, 85
Afghanistan: origin of name, 7; physical features, 7–8, 52–5, 69–70, 117
Afridi tribe, 144
Agriculture, 68, 93*n*., 112, 115, 117–21, 125–7, 131–3
Ahmad Khan: *see* Ahmad Shah Durrani
Ahmad Shah Durrani (Durr-i-Durran), 3–6, 14–16, 17, 29, 137, 144
Airforce, 45, 105
Alauddin Jahansoz, 11
Alexander the Great, 9, 13, 41*n*.
Alexandria Arachosia, 9
Algeria, 22
Ali Khel (scheme), 68, 121
Amanullah, Amir, 30–2, 33, 34*n*., 56, 83–4, 119; reforms, 31–2
Anglo-Russian Convention (1907), 27, 143
Animal husbandry, 119, 125–6
Arabs, 8
Army, 33, 45, 54, 58, 155; administrative, political role, 56, 75–6,

93*n*., 102, 104–5, 113, 115, 119, 132, 164; expenditure on, 131–2
Asoka, 10
Atan (dance), 54
Attlee, Clement, 97
Auckland, 1st Earl of (Gov.-Gen.), 18–19, 23, 143
Aurangzebe, 61
Aviation, civil, 70, 81, 131
Ay Khanum, 9*n*., 40 & *n*.

'Babrak' (politician), 100
Babur, 12–14, 17, 39
Baburnama, 13
Bachha-i-Saqao, 32
Badakshan, 16, 72, 115–16, 129
Baghlan, 48, 123
Bajaur, fighting in, 58
Bakhtar (news agency), 109
Balkh, 11, 111, 124, 129; governor of, *see* Massa
Baluchi tribe, 66
Baluchistan, 16, 27, 51, 55
Bamian, 16, 128; rock carvings, 10
Bangash tribe, 144
Bannu, 143
Barakzai: *see* Muhammadzai Barakzai
Barite, 129
Bedford Company, 44
Bernard, Paul, 41*n*.
Beryl, 129
Birmal, 144
Britain, British, 92, 96, 126, 139; aid, 44, 47, 48, 136; 'Forward policy', *q.v.*; Liberal policy, 19, 20–1, 23–4; relations with A. (*a*) imperial, 17*ff*., 39, 50, 143–4; (*b*) interwar, 30–1, 32, 34, 56, 85; (*c*) post-1945, 35, 37, 48,

173

Britain, British—*cont.*
61–2; *see also* Afghan wars, Imperialism
Buddhism, 10, 88
Bukhara, 143
Burma, 101
Burnes, Alexander, 29
Buzkashi (sport), 71, 74

Cambridge, Duke of, 19
Capital resources, investment, 70, 74, 101, 110, 120, 126, 130–2, 134, 146
Caroe, Sir Olaf, viii, 8, 19*n.*, 25*n.*, 127; Historical Note by, 143–4
Carpets, 78 & *n.*, 125, 126·
Cement, 123
Chadhuri (garment), 37 & *n.*, 77–8
Chagatai, 11
Chahardarra, 78, 126
Chai khanas, 52, 76, 110, 125, 135, 137
Chandragupta, 10
Charikar, 9; massacre at, 18*n.*
China, 8, 17, 25, 42, 45, 46, 51, 63, 138, 139; borders with A., 25, 42
Chitral, 52
Civil rights, 105–6, 151–5
Coal, 129
Coexistence, 136
Communications, 34, 39, 44, 47, 49, 55, 68–70, 115, 127, 130, 131, 134, 153; telephones, 75, 134
Communism in A., 45, 88–9, 100
Constitution (1964), 5*n.*, 82, 85, 87, 90–8, 103, 105–6, 132; text 147*ff.*
Corruption, 94, 97–8, 108, 114
Cotton: cultivation, 41, 47, 121, 125; processing, 44, 47, 48, 68, 122, 123, 124, 130
Currency (afghanis), value of, 43*n.*
Curzon, 1st Marquess (Viceroy), 26
Cyrus, 8
Czechoslovakia, Czechs, 41, 44

Da Afghanistan Bank, 127
Dalbandin, 55
Dari (language), 66, 147

Darius the Great, 9
Daud, Prince, 58, 59, 76 & *n.*, 90, 94
De la Mare, Arthur, 48
Delhi, 14, 15
Demetrius, 10
Democracy, 89, 90*ff.*, 135, 137
Deutscher, Isaac, 43
Dilaram, 47
Disraeli, Benjamin, 22
Doctors: *see* Health services
Durand, Sir Mortimer, 25, 50
Durand Line, 25–6, 33, 34, 40, 50–2, 56, 57, 59, 62, 63, 143–4
Durrani tribe (Abdali), 5, 29, 59, 73, 144
Dust Muhammad, Amir, 5*n.*, 18–19

East India Company, 17
Economy, 43*ff.*, 58, 70–1, 74–5, 101, 117*ff.*; planning of, 101, 128*ff.*, 136
Education, 47, 67, 79, 81, 86, 102, 106, 107, 110, 115, 122, 131, 135, 136–7, 154; madrasah system, 85; *see also* Women
Egypt, Egyptians, 101, 116
Elections, 92–3, 105, 155–6; Shura (1965), 82, 94, 107–9; municipal (1966), 113
Ellenborough, 1st Earl of (Gov.-Gen.), 143
Elphinstone, Mountstuart, 15, 60
Exports, 117, 121, 126–7, 128, 145

Faizabad, 8
Family, 59–60, 76, 78, 80, 97–8, 115
Farhang (politician), 100–1, 102, 103
Ferghana, 12
Fertilisers, 119, 128
First World War, 30
Five Year Plans: First, 130; Second, 39, 75*n.*, 117, 121, 130–4, 146; Third, 66, 121 & *n.*, 132–4
Foreign aid, 110, 123, 124, 126, 129, 131–2, 134, 136; figures, 43–4, 131

Index

Forestry, 48, 68, 121
'Forward policy', 19–20, 22–3, 26–7
France, French, 17, 22, 27, 116, 139
Fraser-Tytler, Sir William, 11
Fruit cultivation, 119, 125, 127

Gandhara, 10
Gardez, 68
Gas, natural, 70, 112, 124, 128; pipeline, 125
Gaugamela (battle), 9
Genghis Khan, 10, 11, 12, 71
Germany, Germans, 27, 34, 35, 41, 115–16, 123, 126; aid, 44, 48, 121, 124, 136, 139
Ghaznavid kingdom, 10–11
Ghazni, 8, 10–11, 13, 15, 143
Ghilzai (Ghalji) tribe, 66n., 73, 144
Ghulam Nabi, 43n.
Gilgit, 27, 52
Gladstone, W. E., 23, 24
Gold, 129
Gorchakov, Prince Aleksandr M., 21
Gypsum, 129
Graeco-Bactrian empire, 9, 10
Greek influence, 9 & n., 53

Habibullah, Amir, 5n., 30
Haidar (minister), 130, 132
Hajigak, 128
Hanafi doctrine, 91, 147, 148, 159, 164
Hartington, Marquess of, 23
Hashim Khan, Sardar Muhammad, 144
Hazara people, 8, 11, 65, 88; character, 71–2; numbers, 66
Hazarajat, 71
Health services, doctors, 67, 68, 80, 105–6, 115, 122, 123, 131, 154
Helmand Valley scheme, 46–7, 68, 121, 131
Herat, 8, 11, 12, 24, 26, 39, 40, 67, 69, 71, 121; siege of (1838), 18
Hindu Kush, 8, 10, 20, 22, 26, 38, 68, 71

Holdich, Sir Thomas, 20, 26, 35
Holland, 22
Humayun, 14
Hungary, 38
Huns, White, 10
Hydroelectric power, 47, 68, 117, 130

Ibn Batuta, 11, 13
Illiteracy, 101–2, 108, 109, 124, 135
Imperialism, British and Russian compared, 27–9
Imports, 117, 127, 145
Income, wages, 75, 80, 81, 120, 122–3
India, 3, 8, 10, 12, 13, 14, 15, 35, 42, 63, 101; relations with A. (a) under Raj, 17ff., 85, 143–4; (b) post-1947, 64, 138 & n.
Indian Mutiny, 22
Indian Ocean, Russian access to, 24, 38, 40, 42, 45, 136
Indus river, 8, 12, 20; waters dispute, 35
Industry, 44, 70, 71, 81, 86, 112, 122–5, 133; see also Manpower, Economy
International Monetary Fund, 44n.
Investment: see Capital resources, Foreign aid
Iran: see Persia
Iron ore, 128–9
Irrigation, 34, 46–7, 68, 112, 117–18, 130, 133
Islam, 9, 10, 65, 83ff., 101; character, influence of, 83–9; and communism, 88; conversion of A., 10–11, 12–87; relations with state, 32, 82–3, 84, 85, 88, 98, 147, 158, 159, 164, 168; status of women under, 31, 76, 82–3
Italy, 32

Jalalabad, 67, 121, 143
Jam minaret, 71
Japan, 34
Judiciary, 96, 114, 163–6; see also Law

Kabul, 8, 11, 12, 13, 15, 30, 33, 38, 41, 46, 47, 69, 71, 123, 143; retreat from (1842), 18*n*.; recaptured, 19, 22; role as capital, 66, 67–8, 75, 167

Kabul Times, 109

Kabul University, 47, 48, 94, 100, 103, 106, 110; *see also* Students

'Kafiristan', 12

Kandahar, 4, 8, 13, 15, 22, 39, 46, 71, 82, 123, 124, 143; airport, 130

Kandahar–Kabul highway, 39, 44, 129*n*.

Karachi, 40, 94*n*.

Karakul skins, sheep, 125, 126–7

Kashmir, 35, 42, 63, 64, 138

Kataghan, 121

Kaufman, General Konstantin P., 21

Khalq (journal), 102–3

Khanabad, 121

Khatak tribe, 144

Khawak Pass, 12

Khiva, 143

Khost, 68, 119–20

Khrushchev, N. S., 58

Khurasan, 9, 16, 143

Khushal Khan (poet), 61, 77

Khwaja-i-Gar, 67, 122

Khyber Pass, 16, 40, 52, 58, 143

Kirghiz steppes, 18

Kochak river, 41 & *n*.

Kohat, 53, 121, 143; arms factory, 60

Koh-i-Noor, 4

Kokand, 143

Koran, 83, 84, 85, 86

Kunduz (town and province), 41*n*., 68, 69, 78, 79, 122, 123; governor of, 107, 112

Kurds, 3

Kushan dynasty, 10

Lalpura, 143

Land ownership, 75, 93*n*., 107, 120–1

Language, official, 66, 147, 154

Lapis lazuli, 129

Lataband Pass, 52

Law, legal system, 57, 86, 105, 106, 114–16, 151–3; *see also* Judiciary

Lawrence, 1st Baron (Gov.-Gen.), 20*n*.

Lead, 129

Lenin, V. I., 32

'Liberal policy': *see under* Britain

Literaturnaya Gazeta, 63

Living standards, costs, 74–5, 133–4

Loya Jirgah, 31, 33, 90, 160–1

Lytton, 1st Earl of (Viceroy), 22–3, 143

Mahipar, 117

Mahmud (Ghaznavid ruler), 10–11

Maiwandwal, Muhammad Hashim, 59, 62, 65–6, 94–5, 97, 99, 103

Majlis, 14

Makran, 8

Malaria campaign, 68, 80, 106

Mangal tribe, 115

Manganese, 56, 129

Manpower resources, skills, 82, 122–5, 130, 133

Marathas, 16

Marble, 56, 129

Marriage, 76, 78–9

Massa, Muhammad Hussein (governor), 111, 112, 124–5

Maurya empire, 10, 14

Mazar-i-Sharif, 8, 67, 68, 69, 70, 111, 121, 128

Menander, 10

Merv, 24

Meshed, 3

Meshrano Jirgah, 90, 93, 96, 107, 155–61; *see also* Shura, Wolesi Jirgah

Military, role of: *see under* Army

Mogul empire, 12, 14, 15, 144

Mohmand tribe, 143, 144

Monarchy, role of, 90–3, 96*n*., 107, 135, 148–51

Mongols, 11, 12, 71*n*.

Morrison Knudsen Company, 46

Muhammadzai Barakzai (clan, dynasty), 5*n*., 9, 29

Mullahs, 30, 31; social, religious influence, 83–7

Index

Municipalities, 113, 166

Nadir Khan; *see* Nadir Shah, King
Nadir Shah of Persia, 3–4, 5*n*.
Nadir Shah, King Muhammad, 5*n*., 33–4, 56, 91, 92, 132, 144
Naghloo, 117
Nangarhar, 68, 117, 129
Nathan Institute, 117*n*.
Natural resources, 34, 48, 56, 117, 124, 128–9, 136
Nesselrode, Count Karl Robert, 18
Nok Kundi, 56
Nomads, 58, 74, 87; character, 72–3; numbers, 66
North-West Frontier, 34, 50, 51, 64; Agency, 33; Force, 54, 57; Provinces, 57
Novosti (journal), 24
'Nuristan', 12

Oil, 124, 129
Orakzai tribe, 144
Outram, Sir James, 20*n*.
Oxus river, 8, 11, 12, 24, 26, 34, 40, 41 & *n*., 44, 68, 71, 118, 122, 136

Pakistan, 35, 38, 39, 42, 53, 55, 69, 70, 73, 88*n*., 121, 137–8; dispute with A., 51, 57–9, 61–4, 132, 138; trade agreement, 40; *see also* Pushtunistan
Paktya, 48, 69, 79, 112, 118–21
Pamir Convention (1895), 25, 26
Pamirs, 25, 26, 42
Panipat (battle), 14
Panjdeh crisis, 24, 30
Pathan people, 7, 8, 13, 26, 50, 65, 88, 113; border areas, 56–7, 58, 132; character, 54, 59–61, 73–4, 113–35; customs, 54, 114–16; dominating role, 66–7, 70, 104, 125, 136; minorities' attitude to, 66, 68, 72, 73, 104, 136
Peace Corps, 46
Persia, Persians, 3, 7, 8, 9, 10, 15, 23, 35, 48–9, 59, 88, 129; influence of, 9, 14, 18, 102, 144
Peshawar, 29, 40, 52, 121, 143

Police, 73, 113–14, 120, 152
Political parties, 93–4, 97, 98–105, 107, 109, 153–4
Population figures, 66
Pottery manufacture, 81, 123
Pottinger, Eldred, 18*n*.
Press, 94*n*., 102–3, 105, 107, 109–10, 130, 153
Property rights, 79, 83, 103, 105, 132, 152–3
Provincial Councils, 91, 93, 113, 114, 156, 160, 166–7
Provincial Governors, 107–8, 112–14
Public Law 480, 47, 129*n*.
Pul-i-Khumri, 123
Punjab, 16, 29
Purdah, 72, 76–7, 78, 81–2
Pushtu, 7, 51, 66, 147, 154
'Pushtun', 7
Pushtunistan, 66, 135, 136, 138; Afghan claim, 50–2, 56, 61–3; Pakistan case, 57, 61–2; hostilities over, 57–8

Qizil Qala, 40
Quetta, 26, 143

Radio, 109, 153; Kabul Radio, 58, 107
Radkan, 3
Ranjit Singh, 17, 18
Ratebzada, Dr Anahita, 82
Rawalpindi, Treaty of (1919), 31
Religious toleration, 87, 147
Revenue, 131–2, 134
Reza Shah of Persia, 31
Rice, 125
Ripon, 1st Marquess of (Viceroy), 23
Roberts, Earl, 19, 26
Royal family, 90, 91–2, 149–51
Russia, Russians, 8, 16; aid, economic, 43–6, 47, 71, 123, 124, 128, 136; aid, military, 45, 131–2; personnel in A., 40–2, 44, 123, 135; in Pushtunistan dispute, 58, 59, 63; relations with A. (*a*) tsarist expansion, 17*ff*., 143; (*b*) interwar, 30, 32, 33–4;

Russia, Russians—*cont.*
  (c) post-1945, 35, 38*ff.*, 49, 63, 138–9; *see also* Imperialism

Sabir Shah, 3, 5
Sabuktagin, 10
Saddozai clan, 19
Safavid empire, 15–16, 144
Salang Tunnel, 39, 68
Samangan, 68
Samanid empire, 10
Samarkand, 12, 143
Saripul, 129
Sassanids, 10
Schlumberger, Dr, 41*n.*
Second World War, 34
Seed-oil, 48, 122
Seleucids, 9
Shah of Persia, 59
Shah Shuja, 19
Shaibani Khan, 12
Shalashak, 129
Shari'at, 28, 79, 159, 164
Sher Shah, 14
Shi'a, 71, 85, 88
Shiberghan, 70, 128
Shura, 82, 83, 90*ff.*, 155–61; *see also* Elections, Meshrano Jirgah, Wolesi Jirgah
Sikh wars, 17
Sikhs, 16, 29, 144
Silk, 119
Simla Convention (1914), 25
Sind, 16
Skobelev, General Mikhail D., 21
Soap-making, 123
Soviet Union: *see* Russia
Spinzar Company, 81, 122, 123
Stalin, J. V., 139
Steel, 70, 128
Students, 103, 106; riots (1965), 73, 94, 100
Sugar, 48, 123
Suleiman mts., 50
Sulphur, 129
Sunni, 71, 84, 85, 88
Supreme Court, 96–7, 164–6

Tajik people, 8, 11, 65; character, 72; numbers, 66

Tamerlane, 12
Tank, 143
Taraqi, Muhammad, 102
Tashkent, 143; conference at (1966), 42
Taxation, 71, 106, 112, 120, 132, 134, 155
Taxila, 10
Termez, 12
Thomson Foundation, 110*n.*
Tibet, 25, 38
Timber, 69, 121
Times, The, 26
Tourism, 51, 127
Trachoma, 106
Trade unions, 122
Transcaspia, 28
Transoxiana, 9
Tuberculosis, 106
Tudeh Party, Persian, 102
Turkey, Turks, 3, 10
Turkmen people, 8, 65, 66

Ulugh Beg, 13*n.*
UNESCO, 106
United States, 22, 35, 38, 39, 42, 47, 49, 123; aid, 44, 46–7, 129 & *n.*, 136, 138; relations with A., 47, 138–9
Unity, problem of, 39, 57, 65–6, 70, 72, 73–4, 88, 104, 132, 135–6
Urchi tribe, 41*n.*
Uzbeg people, 8, 12, 65; character, 70–1; numbers, 66
Uzbekistan, 70, 71

Vietnam, 139

Wakhan, 25
Wardaki, Mrs Mahsuma, 82
Washington, 94*n.*
Wazir tribe, 143–4
Waziristan Scouts, 57
Wheat cultivation, 47, 125
Wilbur, D. N., 66*n.*
Wolesi Jirgah, 82, 90, 92–6, 98–104, 107, 155–61; character, 99–100; *see also* Elections, Meshrano Jirgah, Shura

Women, 31, 47, 65; careers, employment, 78, 80–1, 126; dress, 36, 37–8, 77, 135; education, 67, 79, 106, 137; elected to Shura, 82, 107; social, religious status, 76*ff.*; *see also* Islam
World Bank, 126

Yaftali (minister), 130

Yusuf, Dr Muhammad, 59, 94, 95*n.*, 97, 99, 112, 130
Yusufzai tribe, 59, 144

Zahir Shah, King Muhammad, 5*n.*, 41*n.*, 58, 90, 91; *see also* Monarchy
Zoroastrianism, 88